Introducing Post Modernism and Post Colonialism

By the Same Author

- Contextual Issues: Theological, Ethical and Missiological Responses
- Christian Ethics: Issues and Insight
- Human Rights: Concepts and Perspectives

About the Author

Rev. Dr. M. Stephen obtained degrees of B.A. and M.A (In English Literature) from Kerala University, B.D. and M.Th. from Serampore University. He also received Doctorate in Theology from Dharmaram Vidyakshetram: Pontifical Athanaeum of Philosophy and Theology, Bangalore. Presently he is teaching Theology and Ethics at Faith Theological Seminary, Manakala, Adoor, Kerala. He is a renowned writer and orator having authored several books and published numerous articles in English as well as Malayalam.

Introducing Post Modernism and Post Colonialism

Dr. M. Stephen

CONCEPT PUBLISHING COMPANY PVT. LTD.,
NEW DELHI-110059

ISBN-13: 978-81-8069-931-3

First Published 2013

Published and Printed by

Concept Publishing Company Pvt. Ltd.
A/15-16, Commercial Block, Mohan Garden
New Delhi-110059 (India)
T: 25351460, 25351794, *F*: 091-11-25357109
E: publishing@conceptpub.com, W: www.conceptpub.com
Editorial Office: H-13, Bali Nagar, New Delhi-110 015, India.

Cataloging in Publication Data--*Courtesy:* D.K. Agencies (P) Ltd. <docinfo@dkagencies.com>

Sttīphan, Em.
Introducing post modernism and post colonialism / M. Stephen.
p. cm.
Includes index.
ISBN 9788180699313

1. Postmodernism. 2. Postcolonialism. I. Title.

DDC 149.97 23

Contents

Introduction

Post-modernism and post-colonialism are the major trends in the present context. Post-modernism as an ideology is ecclectic in nature as it is the integration of several elements. Derrida's concept of 'deconstruction' plays a significant role in postmodernism.

According to Willie Thompson, "deconstruction is the practice of submitting texts to post structuralist analysis and extracting from them meanings other than those intended by the author(s), possible entirely opposite ones" (*Post-modernism and History*, New York: Palgrave Macmillan, 2004. p. 129). There is also the concept of 'death of author' related to it, which is based on the argument that the intentions of the author is not important or relevant to the understanding on the meaning of the text. There is also an understanding about the 'play' in signs which makes the meaning of the sign uncertain, as there is no definite meaning to signs. This is the nature of post structuralism and post modernism. For Derrida, the text has no definite or fixed meaning. 'Differance' is another important concept in Derrida's thought. According to Willie Thompson, it is a play on two terms 'differ' and 'defer'. It originates in Ferdinant de Saussure's (structuralist) contention that words derive meaning from the fact that they differ from each other, and in Derrida it is intended to point to the assertion that texts have no foundational meaning and emerge only from the endless play of 'differance', while insisting that 'differance' itself cannot be source of their infinite meanings (*Ibid.;* p. 130). Derrida does not also approve the structuralist division of 'langue' and 'parole', though he favours langue.

Michel Foucault understands power as not hegemonic, but as decentralized. Power is understood not as chanelled throught institutions, but power as a force present throughout the world and in all people. Power is distinct from authority (Mark K. George. "Foucault" *Handbook of Post-modern Biblical Interpretation*, edited by A.K.M. Adam, Missouri: Chalice Press, 2000. p. 92). Knowledge, for Foucault, is received through power. Knowledge also, in his view, sometimes provide subtle way which it controls or regulates people (*Ibid.*, p. 95). Foucault understands, 'archaeology of knowledge' as the uncovering of different categories of discoveries which have prevailed over the span of centuries (Willie Thompson, *op. cit.*, p. 83). He later on prefers the word 'Geneology' which is explained in his book 'power/knowledge and other interviews' as a form of history which can account for the constitution of knowledge discourses, domains of object, etc., without having to make reference to a subject which is either transcendental in relation to the field of events or runs the empty sameness throughout the course of history (cited in Willie Thompson, *op., cit.*, p. 84).

Foucault uses the term 'panopticon' to refer the institution which disciplines the people. It literally means fortress where people are imprisoned. The freedom is curtailed there. Michel Foucault thinks that the social institutions discipline people by using power. It is the 'technology of power'. In our context, we can see the systemic violence in the form of patriarchy and caste system.

Post-modernism does not approve the existing notions and meanings of terms and concept in philosophy, culture and linguistics. It does not go with any structure, so it is post-structural in character. It is based on non-fixity, fragmentation and pluralism. It is also anti-foundational and anti-totalizing. It goes against the meta-narratives. Post-modernism questions the hegemonic understanding of power and knowledge.

Post-colonialism is aware of the ecclectical and opposing elements, so the words 'hybridity 'and 'contrapuntal' (counter point or opposite way) are related to it. Post-colonialism can be an expression which is connected to all that is found after colonialism. But what is more important is what is going on in the colonized countries after colonialisim in relation to social life, politics, philosophy, culture, economics, literature, language, theology and ethics. It is an ideological shift which challenges colonial interests and their superiority claims. It gives importance to what is native and contextual. This hybridity happens in certain countries as there is mixing of races, culture and language. Post-colonialism is also post-structural in nature. It has to resist the colonialism and neo-colonialism. It has to resist what is exploitative and oppressive. The 'imperial interest' and hegemonic spirit are to be rejected.

Dr. M. Stephen
Puthenparambil (Charis villa)
Kaduvakkulam
Poovanthuruth. P.O., Kottayam-12
Kerala

I

Re-Imaging Theology and Philosophy

An epistemological shift is taking place in all spheres. The existing or traditional worldview is totally changed. Pluto was understood as a planet for many years. But now it is found that it is not a planet. Our knowledge and understanding change. Because of the information explosion and the new discoveres our knowledge and understanding widens and also undergoing corrections.

A. Epistemology: An Understanding

It is the theory of knowledge. Knowledge should be more than simple common sense knowledge. According to Jean L. Mercier, "The discoveries made by modern science have compelled us, it seems, to adopt an understanding of the world radically different from the world of our common sense knowledge" (*Epistemology and the problem of Truth*, Bangalore: Asian Trading Corporation, 2000. p. 2). Rene Descartes was critical of the understanding of 'tabula rasa'. There are five trends according to Mercier to classify the view on the problem of knowledge. They are as follows:

(a) *Skepticism*: It argues that the human mind is unable to acquire any legitimate certainties about reality. Wisdom consists in suspending one's judgment on all things and giving us all attempts to understand.
(b) *Empiricism:* It states that the only source of knowledge is experience.
(c) *Rationalism:* It has the view that the only source of knowledge is reason by which man comes to the knowledge of necessary and universal truths.
(d) *Idealism*: It is based on the perspective that the mind only can know its own ideas and has no access to the outside reality.
(e) *Realism*: It has the notion that the human mind is capable of knowing (no skepticism) reality (no idealism) through the use of both experience and reason (neither empiricism nor rationalism) (*Ibid.*, pp. 3-4).

The knowledge is always progressing. According to Mercier, 'our knowledge can never be final, can never come to a standstill' (*Ibid.*, p. 33). Knowledge and transformations in knowledge do occur in history, philosophy, science society, psychology, theology and all areas of life and disciplines. The 'universal' and 'absolute' are being questioned by Nietzsche and Michel Foucault. Post-colonial and post-modern thinking are critical of hegemonicor dominant perspectives in knowledge, power and method or methodology. According to Y.T. Vinayaraj, "post-modernism as an epistemological programme provides new insights on the history of the formation of social space/

self and helps us to initiate counter (epistemologically different) social imaginations on space, position and subjectivity. Subjectivity in the post-modern theory is a self reflexive programme through which one re-position re-locates herself/himself in the current social discourses" (*Re-visiting the other*, Thruvalla: CSS, 2010; p. 15).

B. Re-Visiting the Philosophy

Philosophy is a world-view based on certain pre-suppositions. Each philosophy has its own understanding of morals, life style, view of life and view about society. Philosophy is, etymologically, love of wisdom. Philosophy has a view about reality. Hoernle holds, according to Y. Masih, that 'to philosophise is to seek an attitude towards the universe as a whole'(*A critical history of western philosophy* Delhi: Motilal Banarsidas Publishers, 2006. p. xvii).

Philosophy has a metaphysical formulation. Metaphysical enterprise is not necessarily a scientific attempt. According to Y. Masih, "The language of metaphysics of necessity becomes paradoxical, metaphorical symbolical and analogical" (*Ibid.*, p. xix). They are dealing with concepts like world, god, man, good and bad, and truth. Philosophy has an abstract language and it has a logic of its own. Most of the western philosophy is based on 'either-or' as it excluded the middle. But there is middle ways in Indian philosophical system (e.g. Buddhism and Jainism). Indian system uses the logic 'both-and'. It means a view can be either true or false, and possibility to be both right and false. So there is a middle path.

Western philosophy is based on binary divisions—men and women, good and evil, love and hatred, and sacred and secular. This binary opposites are dealt by post-modernism. This binary opposites, hierarchy and pyramidical gradations are found also in Greek thought and Indian Brahminical systems. They approve the domination and neglect the subaltern. They are elitistic, imperial, exploitative and oppressive in nature. They use power to overpower and disempower others.

Empiricism stresses the fact that knowledge is acquired through sense-experience. Rationalism argues that intellect is an independent source of knowledge (*Ibid.*, pp. xxiv-xxxv). It is important to go beyond the sense-experience and rationalism which are used in a rigid and exclusive sense. Reason has to be also interpreted in the light of historical experience of people. Empiricism also has to consider the historical experience and the reality. Empiricism and rationalism can be exclusively used by the elite or dominant groups in order to degrade and dehumanize the marginated people, as the elites claim to be the custodians of 'true' and 'valid' knowledge. If the elites (e.g. Brahmins) only has an access to 'Brahmavidya', that rationality and knowledge have to be radically challenged. Knowledge can be acquired also from the historical experience and traditional wisdom of the subaltern people and their resources. Kantian understanding of 'a priori' reduces the reason and knowledge to a level of intuition. Reason has to be related to historical experience and knowledge.

In the pre-socrative era, there were theistic and materialistic schools of thought. For materialist, matter is the basis of the universe. *'Virtue is knowledge' is the perspective of Socrates (469-399B.C.).* 'Know thyself' is another important idea of Socrates. According to Y. Masih, "of course, knowing one's own self meant for Socrates, the analysis of knowledge for determining the universal validity of moral principles, laws of the state and the nature of religious faith" (*Ibid.*, p. 30). The method of Socrates was dialogical or conversational. He was critical of the systems and followed the method of questioning and answering, which can be referred as dialectic (*Ibid.*, p. 40). According to Masih, Socrates claimed that real knowledge of justice, virtue, eternal ideas are present in man and it can be recollected by skilful questioning (*Ibid.*, p. 41). Knowledge is dormant as it is, for him, mystic. This is only one aspect, as there is experiential and historical aspect of knowledge. He had a very exclusive view on knowledge as found in dominant religious and philosophical traditions. For Socrates, the knowledge is more intuitive and he thinks that concept of absolute ideas or universals is in the mind and this is not to be found in the observed particulars. He also, states Masih, makes a sharp distinction of sense and reason, and favours reason (*Ibid.*, p. 45) Socrates argues that the colourless, shapeless, intangible realm of thought can be grasped only by reason (*Ibid.*, p. 45).

Plato (428-347 B.C.), was a disciple of Socrates. Ideas are, for Plato, substances. Idea is in and of itself, in Plato's view. Ideas are universal and eternal. They are not perishable, so immutable. Each idea is one and unique.

Ideas are the absolute, so they are invisible and constant. Ideas are the essence of things, for Plato (*Ibid.*, pp. 58-59) Plato respected the community of women and children. There should be promotion of justice in the ideal state. Plato considers education to be the highest blessings for mankind. In his view education should start even when the child is in the womb. He recommends female education (*Ibid.*, pp. 68-69) Plato advocates for common property, as he was against individual property. So his view is closer of communism, as property belong to the community (*Ibid.*, pp. 70-71). According to Y. Masih, Plato denounces both democracy and tyranny as in these systems justice is the advantage of the stronger (*Ibid.*, p. 72). In Masih's view, Plato maintains, that there is one absolute God who is righteous who moves all things in the universe (*Ibid.*, p. 79). In Plato's view, man is responsible for evil. Plato questions hegemonic forces who misuse the power which creates injustice and inequality.

Aristotle (384-322 B.C.) was a disciple of Plato. He was a scientist, logician and thinker. He realized the importance of both inductive and deductive logic in acquiring knowledge (*Ibid.*, p. 84). Plato gave importance to universals and separated it from particulars, but Aristotle thinks that universals cannot exist without particulars (e.g. cowness does not exist anywhere except in individual cows). For him both universals and particulars are integrated (*Ibid.*, p. 89). For Aristotle, change or movement is an important thing, but Plato's view is static. Aristotle thinks that no essence of anything can be outside of it, but for Plato ideas are in the Intelligible world away from the things which belong to the world of becoming. Ideas, for Plato, are static and immobile, which goes against the dynamic view of change of Aristotle (*Ibid.*, pp. 91-92). Aristotle was trying to solve the problem of being and becoming. The nature of knowing, for Aristotle, is to know the cause (*Ibid.*, p. 92). Knowing is through causes (scientific knowledge) and through metaphysical knowledge (wisdom). Science is considered by him as the highest knowledge (*Ibid.*, p. 92) According to Y. Masih, Aristotle developed a doctrine of unfoldment which states "All things are caught up in development form less developed form to higher developed form" (*Ibid.*, p. 96).

Aristotle approves the hierarchical order. There is gradation in his thinking. Rulers are on the top. Then lords, then ordinary citizens, then women and children, and at the bottom, the slaves. In his view, according to Masih, individual man is subsumed under species 'man' and man is subsumed under Animal, as man is highest class 'animal', and animal is subsumed under creature (*Ibid.*, p. 97). Aristotle's pyramidal scheme paved the way for divisions and hierarchical orders—the higher and lower order of things. It leads to dualism and degradations and discriminations.

Rene Descartes (A.D. 1596-1650), was a French man. He attempted, according to Masih, to understand the method of mathematics which could be utilised for advancing knowledge in any subject (*Ibid.*, p. 199). His thinking is based on the dictum 'I doubt or think, therefore I exist'(Cogito ergo sum). One of his principles is never to accept anything as true unless I clearly know it as such.

According to Masih, "Descartes believes that errors arise from poorly comprehended experiences or from hasty, groundless and preconceived notions. The only remedy, therefore, he thinks, lies in resolute refusal to believe in what is not clearly and distinctly perceived" (*Ibid.*, p. 200).

Descartes proposes to begin with simplest objects and ascend, step by step to the more complex. In the words of Masih, for Descartes the explanation must be ordered and systematic. He is in favour of deductive use in philosophical thinking, for he implies that later steps should be clearly deducible from earlier ones (*Ibid.*, p. 200). 'Cogito ergo sum' means consciousness is the means of revealing to our self, something is existing so thinking guarantees our existence (*Ibid.*, p. 202). There are different views on ego or self. Descartes believes that Ego (I think therefore I am) can be known with certainty and John Locke also thinks that self can be known by intuition, but Kant has the opinion that transcendental subject can never be the subject of knowledge as permanent self can never be known empirically (*Ibid.*, p. 203). Descartes is a rationalist as he argues that reason is the sole arbiter of philosophical dispute (*Ibid.*, p. 214). He is also a dualist as he believes that mind and body are two independent substances (*Ibid.*, p. 215).

Benedict de Spinoza (1632-1677) was a jew (born in Amsterdam), originally named as Baruch Spinoza. His main works were 'Ethica', "The principles of the philosophy of Descrates' and 'Treatise concerning God and Man'. Spinoza argues for the unity of all that exists. According to Masih, in Spinoza's view, "A thing apart from its connections with any other thing is an abstraction and unreal on that account" (*Ibid.*, p. 221). So in order that a thing to be true, in Spinoza's perspective, it must follow from the whole reality (*Ibid.*, p. 221). God is, for him, infinite, immutable and eternal intellect. The universe is understood as rational and intellectual. According to Masih, for Spinoza, "God himself being logical or rational allows things to follow from him with intellectual necessity" (*Ibid.*; p. 221).

Spinoza was using a geometrical method, which was indirectly, it is observed by Masih, responsible for his pantheism. In Masih's words," In geometry there is only one presupposition of the single reality, namely, space and all other lines, planes and solids are but modifications of that all-embracing space. Similarly, according to Spinoza, there is only one reality, namely, God and all other things are but modifications of that reality" (*Ibid.*, p. 222). Spinoza understands the world in geometrical form and made it static. It denies the freedom of will because of geometrical reasoning (*Ibid.*, p. 223). The varied experiences of life are to be considered by any philosophy, which is missing in Spinoza's method. The *a priori* nature of geometry does not consider the empirical truth. It is universal in nature, so it ignores the actual state of affairs (*Ibid.*, p. 224). As geometry is very abstract, Spinoza's philosophy is also very abstract in nature. For him, substance is one, infinite, self-caused and eternal reality from which all things follow (*Ibid.*, p. 227). Substance is God, in his view, and God is *Causa sui* or self-creative. He thinks that God creates out of pre-existent matter, states Masih (*Ibid.*, p. 227).

Gottfried Wilhelm Leibnitz (1646-1716) was born in Germany. His law of continuity is based on the generalization of property of numbers, that they can be continued without end and divided without limit, states Masih (*Ibid.*, p. 246). In his view there is no abrupt changes, but every change is followed by another. According to Masih, 'This law of continuity from the highest to the lowest was firmly established in his thought and he was credited to believe that lines were generated by the movement of points, surfaces by the movement of lines and solids by the movement of surfaces" (*Ibid.*, p. 247).

In the law of individuality, Leibnitz recognizes the reality of parts. For him, 'parts in order to be real parts must be as real as the whole of which they are parts. Each part somehow must be the whole and contains the whole. The insistence on the reality of individual things made him believe in pluralism, states Masih (*Ibid.*, p. 247). In the principle of harmony, according to Y. Masih, he maintained that everythings is real for it contains the whole and in some sense is a whole, i.e., a unity within itself (*Ibid.*, p. 247). Leibnitz was highly influenced by mathematics discipline. He was trying to reconcile mind and body, animate and inanimate. Atoms, for him, are dead particles of matter and our own self which is living and spiritual. In his view, states Masih, real elements must be spiritual and Leibnitz calls these indivisible, self-active and spiritual units as monads (*Ibid.*, p. 249). Leibnitz also talks about an epistemology which is mathematical or geometrical. In his perspective, there are two kinds of truth involved in knowledge—necessary and contingent. Necessary truths, in his view, are eternal and unchangeable as they follow mathematical certainty or axioms of geometry (*Ibid.*, p. 2540). It cannot be altered. The necessary truths are abstract and contingent truths are concrete in Leibnitz's view (*Ibid.*, p. 255). He was also trying to say that knowledge does not consist in experience alone, as many elements in knowledge which could not be derived from experience, says Masih (*Ibid.*, p. 258).

John Locke (1632-1704) was born at Somerset, England. His main work was 'Essay concerning Human Understanding'. In his view, knowledge proper is certain instructive and real (*Ibid.*, p. 265). It is observed by Masih that Locke was more concerned with knowing than with the things known. Knowledge should be also instructive as opposed to trifling information (*Ibid.*, p. 265). His view on 'idea' is important to understand his perspectives. The idea has two meanings (1) it may mean a mode of individual consciousness. As such it becomes a subjective modification without any necessary reference to objective things. (2) or else an idea may mean a representation of something other than itself (*Ibid.*, p. 266). According to Y. Masih, Locke was using the term in both senses. Locke admits, states Masih, the presence of the natural faculties, but not innate ideas (*Ibid.*, p. 267). Locke is an advocate of empiricism as he argues that knowledge is obtained not by having innate ideas, but by having clear and distinct ideas through experience (*Ibid.*, p. 268).

George Berkeley (1685-1753) was the Bishop of Clyone and was a native of Ireland. His main works are 'Commonplace Book', New theory of vision' 'Principles of

Human knowledge' and 'Three Dialogues'. His spirtualism or understanding of the reality of God went against materialism. He holds that there is a real world independent of any human subject (*Ibid.*, p. 308). The real world, for him, is strong, lively, orderly, coherent and knit together with laws of nature but the world of fancy is charecterized by fleeting ideas, loosely connected and has arbitrary order of ideas (*Ibid.*, p. 308). His empirical perspective argues for the real world.

David Hume (1711-1776) is a positivist and his works include 'A Treatise of Human Nature', 'An enquiry concerning human understanding and enquiry concerning natural religion'. He makes a distinction between impressions and ideas as impressions are prior and ideas are posterior (*Ibid.*, p. 316). According to Masih, for Hume there can be no simple ideas without their corresponding original impressions (*Ibid.*, p. 316). He rejects the concept of innate ideas. He was against mathematicising efforts of philosophers, as he thinks that mathematical certainty with regard to factual propositions cannot be obtained or demonstrated (*Ibid.*, p. 319). He also held that man is not guided by reason alone, but also by nature, customs and habits (*Ibid.*, p. 319). Hume was an empiricist and positivist as he denies the self, God and permanent substance (*Ibid.*, p. 329).

Immanuel Kant (1724-1804), the German philosopher believed in the validity of scientific knowledge and moral goodness (*Ibid.*, p. 330). According to Y. Masih, for Kant, Knowledge proper is obtained by ordering, connecting and synthesizing them into some system (*Ibid.*, p. 331). Kant has rejected both rationalism and empiricism as they have failed to explain knowledge because they are based on the common assumption concerning the status of objects (*Ibid.*, p. 333). Kant feels that reason must approach nature not as a pupil but as a judge. For Kant, Knowledge is a joint venture of sense and understanding, states Masih. Knowledge begins with sense proceeds then to understanding and ends in reason (*Ibid.*, p. 335). In Kantian view, any epistemology should have occupied itself with the enquiry of *a priori* elements involved in knowledge (*Ibid.*, p. 335). These elements are independent of experience. The rationalism and empiricism are dogmatic systems in Kantian view. So transcends by reconciling these two. For him, in knowledge sense-experience is moulded and transformed by the *a priori* elements contributed by the mind (*Ibid.*, p. 337). Transcendentalism of Kant points out the importance of *a priori* elements in knowledge (*Ibid.*, p338). Kant was giving importance to *a priori* elements in knowledge, than experience and empirical aspect in knowledge. He emphasizes the significant role of *a priori* than a *posteriori*. His main works include, 'critique of Pure Reason', 'Critique of practical Reason' and 'Critique of Judgement'.

George Wilhelm Friedrich Hegel (1770-1831) was a German philosopher. Hegel's idealism is rooted in the dialectic method in which the Absolute unfolds itself through the triple steps of thesis, antithesis and synthesis (*Ibid.*, p. 401). Idealism, according to Masih, is a metaphysical doctrine which asserts the supremacy of the spirit over matter. The spirit can be interpreted as the 'self-conscious mind' (*Ibid.*, p. 402). In Hegel's view, the concrete Universal or the Absolute idea is a system of which the individual, the tribe and nation are inter-related parts. For him, the whole universe consists of ideas which are inter-related in a coherent, rational system. This means that one has to understand the relation which one element has with another and the whole (*Ibid.*, p. 411). Freedom plays an important role in Hegel's thinking. His main works include 'The History of philosophy', "The phenomenology of the spirit', 'The science of Logic,' Lectures on the philosophy of Religion".

According to Y. Masih, 'Reality for Hegel is that which is eternal, unchangeable and a systematic whole' (*Ibid.*, p. 421). The key concept of Hegel, according to Masih, is identity-in-difference or difference-in-identity (*Ibid.*, p. 422). According to Masih's analysis, Hegel's Absolute Idealism has only one Reality. It is all-inclusive and independent. The Hegelian idea is 'many-in-one' or 'one-in-many' (*Ibid.*, p. 423). According to Hegelian dialectics, world contains many changes and these changes are not accidental. He sees the world as dynamic as he took seriously the evolutionary process (*Ibid.*, p. 431). In Hegel's view, history is process and development takes place as there is dialectics between the opposites (The thesis, anti-thesis and synthesis). The dialectics between Being and non-Being is leading to becoming. Becoming includes Being and non-Being. Spirit is a key notion for Hegel and the Absolute is the world-spirit and at work in the form of dialectic process, states Masih (*Ibid.*, p. 433). According to

Hegel, there is nothing arbitrary, accident or chance product in history (*Ibid.*, p. 449).

Karl Marx (1818-1883) was a German philosopher, whose perspectives were based on economic determinism. Against the idealist interpretation of Hegel, he formed a materialist basis. Marx realized the socialibility of man and the dialectic relationship. His epistemology is based on historical consciousness and the development takes place in history though class struggle. He found exploitation and feudalism as the basis of capitalism. Marxism was a revolt against the bourgeoisie. It rejects selfish individualism and looked forward a socialistic society or classless society where everyone is equal. The dictatorship of the proletariat is the focus of Marxism. Marx was conscious of the structural evil found in feudalism and the industrial society. He understands that the working class was exploited by capitalists. Marxism stands for justice and fair wages and rights of the labour class or the poor. The subalterns are the extreme concern in Marxian view. It is also a materialistic philosophy which is anti-religious and atheistic like lokayata philosophical tradition of India.

Francis Herbert Bradley (1846-1924) is from England and he is known as an idealist philosopher. His works include. The pre-suppositions of critical history 'Ethical studies', 'the principles of logic' and 'Appearance and Reality'. Bradley, according to Masih, thinks that knowledge of self is not the clearers or paradigm of knowledge as the self has contradictions so it cannot serve as a model of knowing Reality (*Ibid.*, p. 455). Truth is only an aspect of reality for Bradley. Following Hegel, Bradley calls Reality the 'spirit', and he feels that outside spirit, there cannot be any reality. Spirit, for him, is an organic whole, where the whole is immanent in each of its parts (*Ibid.*, pp. 455-456).

To Bradley, the Absolute Reality is super-relational, so he rejects both internal and external relation. Plurality of facts in daily life are only, for him, appearances of reality. So his system demonstrates that Reality is one all-comprehensive, all-harmonious, sentient whole (*Ibid.*, p. 460). For him, reality is a sentient experience. To be real, in his view, is to be indissolubly one thing with sentience. In this integral sentience there is no separation of subject and object, self and not-self (*Ibid.*, p. 463).

The philosophies which are discussed in this section are having their own particular ideological stance. They have their own world-view and epistemology. Most of these philosophies, except philosophies like Marxism, are very abstract, intuitive and elitistic and are nothing to do with the issue of the people which are contextual. The affirmation of hierarchy based on class system, extreme individualism and capitalistic tendencies of western context are reflected in most these philosophies.

C. Re-Imaging of Theology

Traditionally, theology is also a reflection of western philosophy, which is very abstract and elitistic. These Philosophies and theologies ignore or are discriminatory towards class and gender issues. They affirm the hierarchical orders of the society which is based on natural philosophy. There was no challenge or epistemological shift until the emergence of political theologies. The classical theologies are not very historically conscious as the people's issues are ignored. Most of them were captives of Greek philosophical system, which is based on reason, formalism and mathematics. The structuralism of traditional philosophy and theology are being challenged.

The early church fathers have tried to link Christian thought with Greek philosophy. Their theologizing was apologetical and philosophical in nature. Justin Martyr (100-165 A.D.) was trying to equate Christ with logos as we see in apostle John, by way of relating Christianity with Greek philosophy or philosophical world of the time.

According to Battista Mondin, "In Justin's opinion, every man, in so for as he has reason, participates in some way in divine Reason (the enternal "Logos") which is a universal principle of rationality. Therefore, every man has the capacity to gather some fragment of truth, a truth which Christ only has allowed us to know in its entirety" *(A History of Medieval Philosophy*, Bangalore: TPI, 2005. p. 19) Justin's concept of 'logos spermatikos', is famous. He believes that the all-pervading spirit of logos is found everywhere, and it works in all human beings and enlightening them.

Clement of Alexandria's (Born C. 150 AD and died C. 215 AD) perspective is also apologetic in nature, as he was attempting to defend Christianity from Gnostics and to give, according to Mondin, 'a logical and rational (philosophical) structure to Christian doctrines (*Ibid*., p. 21). Clement of Alexandria sees philosophy as preparation for the Gospel. He stated," What the Law was for the Jews, philosophy was for the gentiles until the coming of Jesus" (*Ibid*., p. 23). According to Clement, the only author of any truth is God, and it is by the means of philosophy that the Greeks travelled a part of the road to arrive at Christ (*Ibid.*, p. 5). According to Mondin the argument of Clement is that philosophy is incapable of causing salvation, while faith is indispensable for salvation (*Ibid.*, p. 18). According to Mondin, there was an attempt to hellenize Christianity as Christianity is called the philosophy and Christ is called the "Logos", and God is also referred as "Logos" as the supreme Being and the prime cause (*Ibid.*, p. 36). The attempt of Clement was to rationalize Christianity.

Origen, the disciple of clement of Alexandria, was born around 185 AD, probably in Alexandria (*Ibid.*, p. 59). He died around 253 AD. Origen supports the close relationship between Christianity and philosophy. For Origen, even before Christ's incarnation, philosophy prepared the Greeks to understand and accept the word ("Logos") of revelation (Ibid., p. 60).

Augustine was born on 354 AD in Tagaste (Modern Algeria). He was reacting to Manicheans and Pelegians. Pelagius argued that sin is a voluntary act and it will not cause any damage to posterity, or he believes that sin is not inherited. Augustine questioned this view and taught that sin is inherited and it deprives man of the correct use of free will (*Ibid.*, p. 111). Augustine believes in the total depravity of man. His view of cosmos and history is based on two cities, the terrestrial city and heavenly city. He has a dualistic understanding of what is sacred and what is secular or profane. According to him, terrestrial city includes the universe of evil, and celestial city includes the universe of good (*Ibid.*, p. 123).

Gregory of Nyssa was a significant person in eastern patristics. He was born in Nyssa around 335 AD. In the doctrinal explanations, he used the philosophical reasoning. He concludes that God is unknowable (*Ibid.*, p. 137). He sees God as ineffable or untraceable (*Ibid.*, p. 138). According to Mondin, in Gregory's view God's essence cannot be known properly, but God can be known by his operations. So he is closer to Aristotelian logic, that it is impossible to discuss the infinite (*Ibid.*, p. 139). God is very abstract in the perspectives of Gregory of Nyssa.

Anselm of Aosta (1033-1109) relates faith and reason in his theology, which is expressed through the words 'Credo untelligam' (I believe in order to understand). According to Mondin, "This aphorism evidences two things: first the necessity of faith in the knowledge of religious and moral truths (hence the importance of the credo"); the second, the necessity of using reason, so that the adhesion of faith may not be blind and simply passive (hence the importance of the intelligam") (*Ibid.*, p. 248).

Peter Abelard (1079-1142) Peter Abelard was born at Palais (Brittany). According to Mondin, "In Abelard, reason detaches itself from faith and treats it as an equal" (*Ibid.*, p. 257). He was concerned of solving the problem of universals.

Thomas Aquinas (1225-1274): Incorporates Aristotle's philosophy in Christian thought. He uses philosophical categories in his theology such as 'being' and 'essence'. Reason also plays a dominant role in his theology. He portrays God as the unmoved mover. The ontological and transcendental dimension of God is stressed. Knowledge is understood by Aquinas as intellectual in nature. He feels that reason has the ability to know the existence of God. The natural law has influenced the theology of Aquinas.

Abstract categories are found in most of the western theologies and theologians. Scheleiermacher, Karl Barth, Bultmann and Paul Tillich were using western categories to explain the theology. They stressed the abstract, transcendental and ontological dimension of God. 'Being' and 'essence' are found in their theological formulations. The existential, dialectic or apologetic nature of theologies are abstract and not very much concerned of concrete issues. Some of the modern theologians are actively responding to social and political issues, but were sometimes victims of western framework, so they were not dealing the issues in a concrete manner. Some concrete expressions, to an extent, come out from Dietrich Bonhoeffer as he was dealing with the political evil of the time.

Most of these theologians have developed a theology from above as they depend so much on the existing philosophies or ideologies, and their theory of knowledge did not consider the experiences and tradition of the marginated. An epistemological shift is found in present political theologies.

D. Re-Assessment and a Re-Imaging of Philolosophy and Theology

The western theologies are oriented mostly in western philosophy, economics, sociology and culture. They may also have a domineering and colonial spirit. They are elitistic in nature. The western framework is also very abstract, which is uncritically used by theologians in their formulations. Western philosophies are highly hierarchical in nature, so they affirms gradations and discriminations as they are rooted in natural law, which deny the value and dignity of the marginated like women, children and the labour class. They are not concerned of people who live in ghettoes, who are subalterns. This nature of philosophy is also reflected in western theologies. Experiences of the poor are not considered in western philosophies and theologies. Most of the empirical realities are ignored by them.

The philosophies and theologies of the west have developed a 'system' which is classical, closed, and abstract which is challenged by post-modernism and post-colonialism. Deconstruction became the key word in re-imaging philosophies and theologies. The existing parameters of 'knowledge' and theories are being questioned. The subaltern consciousness has impacted to have a new understanding on realities. The feminism, dalit and tribal awakening have created a new awareness in theology. The worldviews, experiences, traditions and expression of the maginated groups are considered in theologizing today. The voices of the victimised, the suffering of third world people, their culture and socio-political experience are a great concern in theology today. The subaltern, victimized and oppressed are the 'other' who are powerless, who are to be the central concern in our theologizing.

There is epistemological shift as we see the influence

of post-modernism and post-colonialism. The authorities and traditions are undergoing challenges. The reason is replaced by experience especially of the subalterns. The elitistic traditions like the Brahminic and western are also being challenged by the subatterns. The sources of authority are now considered from the dalits, tribals, blacks and other victimized groups. Their historical consciousness and traditions, religiosity, culture and experiences are considered as very valuable and they are very much used in the making of theology. A de-legitimation or deconstruction is taking place in every sphere. The monolithic structures, ideologies, philosophies and theologies are undergoing criticism as they are not considering the issues of the context and people. The classical form of epistemology is being challenged by the people from margins. The dominant class and their views and pre-suppositious are questioned by the marginalized.

II

Post-Modern and Post-Colonial Context

The French Revolutionary Rousseau said, 'man is born free, but everywhere he is in chains'. Mankind is bound to different kinds of slavery—physical and intellectual. The powerful, imperial and colonial structures physically and intellectually (ideologically) attempts to enslave the powerless. The powerful always think that the right and wrong in relation to law, knowledge and behaviour is their own monopoly. The people of the occident had the opinion that the people of the orient are inferior physically and intellectually. The occident does not like to recognize the dignity, rights, traditions, wisdom and the creativity of the orient. There is a spirit of dominance or imperial spirit which is found in every relationship in all spheres of life.

A. Post-Modern Context

There is no unanimous opinion about the beginning of post-modernism, as the elements of post-modernism are found in different period of time. In an organized sense the spirit of post-modernism is found in 1930's. It is observed that the 'post-modernism' is first surfaced in 1934 in the Spanish writer Frederico De Onis. It is also indicated that the term 'post-modernism' is appeared in the intellectual scene with the publication of American periodical 'A Journal of post-modern culture and religion' in 1972. Post-modernism is however a radical departure from the modern worldview and thinking. Defining postmodernity or post-modernism is a difficult task. Postmodernity is the state or condition, and post-modernism is the ideology. Post-modernism is the ideology which affirms the relativism, pluralism, contextuality, liberation and deconstruction. It goes against meta-narratives and hegemony. It challenges the power structures. Colonialism, imperialism and dominance are questioned by post-modernism.

Post-modernism does not approve any centre so it is for centrelessness. The features of post-modernism are also recognized as rapidity, indeterminacy chaos, disorder, secularism, openness, rejecting the absolutes, anti-foundationalism and post-structuralism. Fragmentation is another nature of post-modernism. It is anti-hierarchical and anti-totalizing.

In the post-modern context, everything is undergoing changes in rapid speed. In the post-modern world, one can only be a spectator of what is going on. In this context, there is ample freedom for people to act according to their choice. The existing notions, ideals and practices are being challenged and undergoing changes. Marriages are gay and lesbian, studies are online (no classrooms), room keys appears in the form of a card or number (electronic), doors of the vehicles are open by remote control system, buildings look like a fallen structure, music comes in the form of pope and rock and poem is written in prose. Everything can be in a fluid situation, even as traditional values are not regarded so also the traditional understanding of power and authority.

B. The Post-Colonial Context

Post-colonialism is an ideology that questions the forces of colonialism. It also makes protest against domination, hegemony and power. It stands for nationalism, nativity and indigeneity. It challenges the spirit of colonialism and neo-colonialism (globalization). Post-colonialism promotes freedom and liberation. Post-colonialism gives importance to the native tradition, wisdom and perspectives. It challenges the claims of the occident, which affirms the superiority of west in all spheres of life, and affirms the contribution of the orient. There is strong ideological conflict against colonial spirit in post-colonialism. As in post-modernism, post-colonialism rejects the hegemonic forces. It goes against the oppression and systemic violence which are found in socio-political and religio-cultural realms.

The post-colonial ideology was a reaction to colonialism in Asian continent or third world context and elsewhere. The European powers such as Portughese, Spaniards, French and the British were quite interested in colonizing other countries in order to exploit and oppress them politically and economically. It involves uprooting the people, destroying their traditions, values and plundering their resources.

The movements or struggles for independence were taking place in the colonized third world and they were demanding autonomy or self-rule and freedom. The aim was to de-colonize that brings results in 1940's, 50's and 60's. Many Asian and Latin American countries have attained freedom from the colonial powers. The native people have suffered a lot from the colonial powers. They were brutally treated. The western powers have attempted to annihilate many aboriginals like Red Indians and Maoris. Uprooting the indigenous people from their culture and religion was one of the main attempt of colonial powers. The emergence of subaltern consciousness (study of their history, culture and traditions) is also one of the main contributions of post-modernism and post-colonialism.

III

Post-Modern and Post-Colonial Philosophy

Medieval and modern are the context of post-modernism. Post-modernism challenges the modernism. Post-colonialism begins at the end of colonialism. Post-colonial thinking began even before it as a reaction to colonialism. There is no unanimous opinion about the beginning of post-modernism.

A. Post-modern Philosophy

Modernism is the 18th century development of enlightenment. Modernity is the intellectual and cultural heritage of enlightenment project. Enlightenment and modernism emphasize the humanism. Enlightenment means, in the level of thought, emotions and will there is no need of external force—teacher, revelation or scripture. Immanuel Kant gave importance to freedom, intuition and conscience. Liberalism and humanism are the contributions of enlightenment.

Modernity rejects the authority of tradition, religion and culture. It supports the secular view. It questions the conventional wisdom. The nature of enlightenment are four.

(1) Human Freedom

According to Immanuel Kant, human freedom is living by human will without the dictate of external commands. It is a mature living. Rene Descartes affirms that 'I think, so I am'. Cartesian ego promotes the human autonomy. For modernism, if our will is dependent, we are not mature and our existence, as existentialism states, is not authentic. The dictum is 'think boldly' (Sapere Aude). Each human being thinks that he/she is sovereign of himself or herself. It does not give importance to God (what is supernatural), scripture, or tradition. Modernism has rejected the church leadership, and theology.

(2) Supreme Power or Sovereignty

Modernism reject the external authorities and depends on reason (Kant). Kant talks about pure reason (which discerns subjects and facts or objects) and practical reason (which will help to know how we can function or work suitably). Modernism is for autonomy than heteronomy.

(3) Modern Science and Technology

Human beings think that they have potentiality to control the whole world. They feel that they can regulate the world by the help of science and technology. There is no theocracy but technocracy. Industrialization, telecommunication and development are the elements of this factor. Science and technology do not give importance to the divine.

(4) Secular State

The 'Sacred' is kept away. The French revolution had also contributed so much to secularism. It puts foreward the principle by which state is different from religion. The western enlightenment rejects God as an unnecessary hypothesis.

Post-modernism questions the intuitive understanding. Michel Foucault (1926-1984), French post-modernist thinker questions what is enlightenment from within. Freedom is rejecting the idea of enlightenment from within. It is a post-enlightenment culture. Foucault is arguing for relativism. He said that we can say and write many things, but can't be proved. He is called as antinomian, nihilist and anarchist.

Post-modernism is an epistemic shift in thinking and perspectives. It is the outcome of a new understanding and knowledge. Charles Olson refers post-modernism to indicate the poetry and poetic style which is not man-centred. While modernism is man-centred, post-modernism is not man-centred. Infact, there is no particular centre for post-modernism. Post-modern society is depicted as media society, electronic society, information society and consumeristic society. Post-modern worldview is based on iconoclasm or deconstruction and this is found in art, literature and theology. It is against institutionalization of art, song, story etc. The old songs are given new version and style. In post-modernism, art is not a mirror of reality, but it is a forged document which speaks to our life. Post-modernism supports people-oriented art. It is against classical, and for popular.

Artist, in post-modern thinking, is not the original authoritative author. He is just the one who draws. The appreciator is also participating is the understanding of meaning. Post-modernism is also post-structural as it rejected the idea that language has a structure. Post-structuralism stresses the deconstruction. Post-modernism is a society of spectacles. We are controlled by other forces. We are controlled by market and products. Our values and worldviews and life are undergoing deconstruction. The particular concern is also stressed by post-modernism as it supports localism and contextuality. The Micropolitics, Microbiology, Microeconomics, Peace Movements, Civil Right Movements, Women Movements, Ethnic Movements, Dalit and Tribal Movements, and Ecological Movements are post-modern in nature. The post-modern thinkers also believe that truth or reality is a social construct and this is to be reconstructed or deconstructed.

Postmodernity reacts to modern worldview and stand for a new science, a new spirituality and a new society. Graham Beatie points six shifts in relation to modernism and post-modernism, as follows:

(1) Rational to experiential
(2) Individual to community
(3) Uniformity to diversity
(4) Mechanic to organic
(5) Exclusivism to pluralism
(6) Progress to centrelessness.

Post-modernism affirms experiential, community, Diversity, Rapidity, Non-fixity, Organic, Pluralism and centrelessness. Postmodernity affirms that there are different worlds. There is no given universal centre by which one can build their knowledge or base. It prefers mini or micro-narratives as against grand or meta-narratives. For the subaltern people it is a movement to selfhood and empowerment. Post-modernism emphasizes local, specific and historically informed analysis. It rejected universal and broad generalizations. Foucault said about the 'false hegemonic knowledge' which can be challenged by 'counter hegemonic forces' which can look for alternative explanation, is post-modern (e.g. relating women issues to their self-understanding and empowerment). Jacques Derrida looked for deconstruction of texts (Biblical text and written or oral texts). It is de-legitimization, de-legitimizing the hegemonic centre of knowledge and power (e.g. liberation theology as counter theology).

I. The Key Post-modern Thinkers

(A) Michel Foucault

Foucault was born in poitiers, France in October 15, 1926, and died in Paris, June 25, 1984. He was politically active and stood in support of homosexuals and marginalized and his books are centred around histories of medical and social sciences. His major works are 'The History of Madness in the Classical Age' (1961), 'The Birth of the Clinic (1963), 'Discipline and Punish', 'The Archaeology of Knowledge.' 'The Abnormal', 'The Madness and Civilization' and 'The Order of Things'. Foucault questions the conventional bourgeois morality. He also attacks Phenomenology and

Marxism. He was critical of modern system of disciplinary power. Modern disciplinary society, according to him, is based on three techniques of control: hierarchical observations, normalizing judgement and the examination. The examination is understood by him as the hierarchical understanding of power and knowledge. He also feels that the various modern bodies of knowledge about sexuality have an intimate association with the power structures of modern society and so are prime candidates for genealogical analysis. He also thinks that modern regulation or control of sexuality parallels modern control of criminality by making sex an object of allegedly scientific discipline, which offers knowledge and domination of their objects. He advocated for alter-language or counter-language. In his book, 'It is not a pipe', he discribes the pen as penis and ink as the semen. The process of writing is referred as the sexual act. Foucault rejects the misuse of power by dominant and is concerned of the 'other', the subalterns or marginalized. Foucault, in his book 'Abnormal' depicts how the sick, especially the lepers were treated by the hegemomic force in the Medieval period. The lepers were alienated by the relatives, the society and civil authorities and at last they are ex-communicated from the town. He was making us aware how the powerful are marginalizing the helpless ones.

About power, Foucault rejects the power which is anchored in macrostructures or ruling classes as it is repressive in nature. Power, for him, is heteromorphous, dispersed, productive. He wants to get rid of juridical and negative representation of power and cease to conceive it in terms of law, prohibition, liberty and sovereignty. He was against the negative relation between power and sex, the insistence of rule, the cycle of prohibition and the logic of censorship.

(B) Jacques Derrida (1930-2004)

He was a French philosopher, who was born in EI-Biar, near Algiers which was a French colony. He was influenced by German philosophers such as Edmund Husserl and Martin Heidegger. But he was critical of them. The school of deconstruction was originated from his analytical approach which is applied to literature, linguistics, philosophy, law and architecture. His trilogy—'Speech and Phenomena', 'of Grammatology', and 'writing and difference' are crucial to his framework of deconstruction. His other mains works are, 'Margins of Philosophy', and 'Dissemination'.

He rejected the logocentrism. In his view, writers gave expression to certain essential truths and it is the duty of the reader to search out. According to Derrida, the 'logocentrism' was epitomized in the way in which readers are traditionally encouraged to approach philosophical texts as a bunch of fixed universal truths. For him, status of the text can no longer be determined by its boundaries, where meaning starts or ends. Meanings are never complete. Text, for him, is a complex network of unfinished meanings and text can't be run out by the determinations of a writer's intents of fixing a single meaning.

The notion of deconstruction comes from Martin Heidegger's idea of 'destruction'. Destruct means deconstruct, which does not mean obliteration. It means restructuring. For Derrida, there is no original position from which thinking begins. He speaks of decentring of the structurality of structure. He meant that outside the discourse there is no fixed point which one can establish metaphysical boundaries for linguistic signifiers.

Deconstruction is a method of literary criticism which assumes that language refers to itself rather than to an extratextual reality and which asserts multiple conflicting interpretations of a text and bases such interpretations on the philosophical, political or social implications of the use of language in the text rather than on the author's intention. He proposed the 'death of the author'. The writer has no authority over the meaning of what is written.

Deconstruction of Derrida is described as an approach which rigorously pursues the meaning of a text to the point of exposing the contradictions and internal oppositions upon which it is apparently founded and showing that those foundations are irreducibly complex, unstable or impossible. Derrida applies this approach in philosophy, literary analysis and other fields. It is also stated that deconstruction tries to demonstrate that any text is not a discrete whole but contains several irreconcilable and contradictory meanings; that any text therefore has more than one interpretation, that the text itself links these interpretations inextricably, that the incompatibility of these interpretations is irreducible and thus that as interpretative reading cannot go beyond a certain point. Derrida refers this point as an aporia in the text (http://en, wikipedia org/wiki/Deconstruction). Aporia can mean that the meaning of text is not decidable. In the perspective of J. Hillis Miller, deconstruction is not a dismantling of the structure of a text, but a demonstration that it has already dismantled itself.

A very important concept in Derrida is *differance*. It is a complex term which refers to the process of the production of difference and deferral. In Derrida's view, all differance and all presence arise from the operation of differance. He talks about realm of reality (differance) and realm of identities (of predication and presences). At the level of difference, there is no identities, no fixed or settled meaning. It is the non-cognitive realm. In his view, there is no objective knowledge. All knowledge is contextual and influenced by culture, traditions, prejudices and beliefs.

Literary analysis has looked forward the meaning of the text as the expression of its author's mind. Deconstruction (Derrida) detaches meaning from author's intention. Text is understood as the source of many conflicting or opposite meanings. What the author wrote was always going beyond his/her own intention. Deconstructionalists understand commentary not as the true content of text, but as free elaboration of themes suggested by one text.

Jacques Derrida also distinguishes speech (logos) and writing. In western thought, speech is privileged as the expression of what is immediate and certain, and writing is understood as inferior to speech. Writing is understood as distorted, loss of certainty or absence of presence. This privilege (of speech as pure) of speech over writing is called phonocentrism or logocentrism. Derrida was critical of logocentrism. Deconstruction tries to bring writing as writing to writing. It is a way of recording pure thought to disclose meaning of differance. Language is constantly changing and text has multiple legitimate interpretation. So there is no absolutes in terms of truth or meaning. In Derrida's book of 'Grammatology', he uses deconstruction to discuss the implications of understanding language as writing rather than speech. Derrida opines that when language is understood as writing, it is realized that meaning does not originate in the logos or thought of the language user. Instead, individual language users are understood to be using an external system of signs, a system that exists separately to them because these signs are written down.(http://en.wikipedia.org/wiki/Deconstruction). The deconstruction is more related to anti-structuralism than post-structuralism. But certainly it is post-structural in nature.

Jacques Derrida is critical of logocentrism which supports the determination of the being of the entity as presence (Jacques Derrida, of Grammatology, Delhi: Motilal Banarsidas Publisher's, 1976. p. 12). In the view of Oliver Davies, Derrida's project is to dismantle the western philosophy of presence with respect in particular to Husserl and Heidegger, takes the form of an exposition of differance, which means infinitely deferred and Heidegger, which means infinitely deferred of the meaning (Theology of Compassion, Michigan: William Eerdmans Publishing Co., 2001. p. 123). According to Derrida, Saussure depends on the understanding of Aristotle that spoken words are the symbols of mental experience and written words are the symbols of spoken words. For Saussure, language and writing are two distinct systems of signs; the second exists for the sole purpose of representing the first (*of grammatology*, p. 30). These views give importance to speech or spoken words which Derrida questions. Derrida believes that grammatology is possible by undoing of logocentrism (*Ibid.*, p. 74). According to Julian Wolfreys, 'writing' for Derrida is a metaphor. He is not merely concerned of binary opposition of writing and speech, but concerned of 'differance'. Meaning, for him, is not fixed, but provisional, and always a condition of differance (*Deconstruction Derrida*, Hampshire: Macmillan Press Ltd., 1998. pp. 66-67). Derrida's reading is a challenge to traditional method of reading as it is a different reading.

Joseph Adams states that 'deconstruction' seeks or celebrates limitless interpretation and an unrestricted semantic play (quoted in *Deconstruction Derrida*, p. 33). In an interview, Derrida stated that deconstruction does not consist in a set of theorems, axioms, tools, rules, techniques, methods. There is no deconstruction, deconstruction has no specific object (cited in *Deconstruction Derrida* p. 49).

For Derrida, states Julian Wolfreys, deconstruction not only teaches us to read literature more thoroughly by attending to it as language, as the production of meaning through difference and dissemination, through a complex play of signifying traces. It also enables us to interrogate the covert philosophical and political presuppositions of institutionalized critical methods which generally govern our reading of a text. It is not a question of calling for destruction of such institutions, but rather of making us aware of what we are infact doing when we are subscribing this or that institutional way of reading (this idea is taken from Derrida's 'Deconstruction and other' and cited in *Deconstruction Derrida*, p. 51).

Derrida also stated that it is no longer a question of deconstructing discourses and semantics, but primarily institutional and political structures (*Ibid.*, p. 185). Derrida was critical of the dichotomies and polarities which affirm the hierarchical order. Some of the polarities are, good vs. evil, being vs. nothingness, persence vs. absence, identity vs. difference and speech vs. writing (Jacques Derrida, *Dissemination*, translated by Barbera Johnson, London: The Athlone Press, 1981. p. viii). Derrida criticizes the privileging of the spoken word over the written word by western metaphysics (*Ibid.*, p. ix)

An important concept in Derrida is the 'differance'. According to Derrida, as soon as there is meaning, there is differance. Differance (derives from the French verb 'differe' which means "to differ" and "to defer" or postpone) inhabits the very core of what appears to be immediate and present (*Ibid.*, p. ix) Derrida feels that without the possibility of differance, the desire of presence as such would not find its breathing space (*Ibid.*, p. xi). Dissemination is brought by differance. 'Differance' is a Derridian neologism which means active non-self-presence both in space and time (*Ibid.*, p. 5).

According to Willie Thompson, "Differance is not the originatory point of meaning; if taken seriously the implication of his position is that there is no fixity of meaning (possibly no meaning) and 'differance' is a concept which cannot be conceptualised. It is the mark—or 'trace' as Derrida prefers to say—of a permanent absence" (post-modernism and history, New York: Palgrave Macmillan, 2004, p. 3). For Derrida, deconstruction is the practice of submitting texts to post-structualist analysis and extracting from them meanings other than those intended by the author(s) possibly entirely opposite ones. 'Death of the author concept has the argument that the intentions of the author are irrelevant to the understanding of the meanings of any text. According to Derrida, text has no fixed meaning. In deconstruction, there is a 'play' in signs, which makes the meaning of signs uncertain. There is no definite meaning to signs. This is what post-structuralism or post-modernism, states Willie Thompson, (*Ibid.*, p. 13ff). According to Wolfreys, the identity is recognizable through the play of writing, difference. By identity we mean there is otherness within identity, or even alterity (*op. cit.*, p. 120).

Derrida used the word 'hymen' and a nonsynonymous substitution for the key term 'differance' states Wolfreys (*op. cit.* p. 107). In Wolfrey's view, Derrida used the word 'hymen' with double meaning. It is, for him, a sign of fusion between identities. This figure marks the difference, and also connectedness, between two places, two identities. Hymen, for him, is the graphics expression of the margin, limit or border which connects opposites, binary oppositions such as inside and outside, and allows their meanings to be understood in relation to one another, while reserving to itself a non-determined place for which a univocal meaning cannot be found in the figure of the hymen and interpretative acts cannot control its meaning (*op. cit.*, p. 109).

The Truth in Derrida stands for unveiling. It is non-hiddenness, non-concealedness or disclosure. Derrida's deconstruction goes against the dischotomies or polarities of metaphysics such as presence and absence, good and evil and being and nothingness. Indeterminacy in Derrida means undecidable. It is linguistic indeterminacy. The term differance comes from the French word 'differ' means to defer or to differ. It is a deliberate twisting of the word *difference.* It means that words have different meanings and images. Derrida goes against the synchronic understanding of the terms and concepts. He also questions traditional, hierarchical and dominant understanding/meaning of words. Deconstruction is not a mechanical operation which considers the procedural forms of judgment, so Derrida avoids the word 'method'. As a philosophy, Derrida is useful in re-constructing the hierarchical authority/power, the orders, the misogynist perspectives and the domination of power against the marginated. It traces out binary oppositions like powerful and powerless, and male and female (men or women). Derrida's philosophy challenges any system or framework which centred around a fixed pattern of thinking.

(C) Jean Francois Lyotard (1924-1998)

He was a French thinker. His work includes 'The post-modern condition: A Report on knowledge'. Lyotard understands that post-modern condition rejects metanarratives and it is anti-totalizing. Lyotard uses the word 'anagogy' in order to refer the interpretation of the word or text that finds beyond the literal, allegorical, moral and a spiritual or mystical sense. Anagogy designates a global meaning. He is understood as a first post-structuralist who clearly relates post-structuralism with post-modernism.

He was analysing the post-modern world from a post-structuralist perspective. One of the examples is the commodification of truth. He must have introduced the concept of metanarrative or grandnarrative in post-modern discussion in order to criticize the use of individual liberty or the progress of the speculative spirit in modern era to legitimize knowledge. Lyotard is referring about post-modernism mostly in relation to cultural changes. Meta-narratives are understood by him as two kinds—political and philosophical.

According to Lyotard, the post-modern artist goes beyond the traditional rules and patterns, and he is a philosopher in nature. He states, 'those rules and categories are what the work of art is looking for: The artist and the writer then are working without rules in order to formulate the rules of what will have been done. Hence, the fact that the work and text have the character of an event: hence also they always come too late for their author, or what amounts to the same thing, their being put into work, their realization ....always begins too soon. Post-modern would have to be understood according to the paradox of the future (post) anterior (modo)'.

(D) Jean Baudrillard (1929-)

He was a French postmodernist thinker. His perspective is more nihilistic. The post-modern context is developed, he thinks, by the combination of information technology, telecommunication network and simulations. His main works were 'The mirror of production' 'Simulations' and 'In the shadow of the silent majorities'. The post-modernism, in his view, is represented by implosion and de-differentiation.

He was a critic of modern society and developed a new kind of social analysis. He has challenged classical social theory. He distrusted the dogmatic and reductive nature of Marxism. According to Douglas Kellner, "He also argues that Marxism does not critique capitalist societies radically enough and calls for a more extreme break" (*Post-modernism: The key figures*, edited by Hans Bertens and Joseph Natoli, Massachesetts: Blackwell Publishers Ltd, 2002. pp. 50-51). He argues that we live in the hyperreality of simulations in which images, spectacles, and the play of signs replace the logic of production and class conflict as key constituents of contemporary societies (*Ibid*., p. 52). In this book, 'Symbolic exchange and Death' he opines that modern societies are organized around the production and consumption of commodities, while post-modern societies are organized around simulation and play of images and sign, denoting situation in which codes, models, and signs are the disorganizing principle of a new social order where simulation rules.

In the society of simulation, identities are constructed by the appropriation of images and codes and models determine how individuals perceive themselves and relate to other people (*Ibid.*, p. 52). Douglas Kellner understands that, "Baudrillard's post-modern world is also one of radical *implosion*, in which social classes, genders, political differences, and once-automous realms of society and culture collapse into each other erasing previously defined boundries and differences" (*Ibid.*, p. 52). In Baudrillard's view post-modern societies are characterized by dedifferentiation or implosion. In his view, in the society of simulation, economics, politics, culture, sexuality, and the social implode into each other, states Kellner (*Ibid.*, p. 52).

Baudrillard's post-modern world is one of *hyperreality*. It is a world in which entertainment, information, and communication technologies provide experiences more intense and involving than the scenes of banal everyday life. According to Douglas Kellner, "The realm of the hyperreal (i.e., media simulations of reality, Disneyland and Amusement Parks, malls and consumer fantasy Parks, TV Sports, and other excursions into ideal worlds) is more real than real, whereby the modes, images, and codes of the hyperreal came into control thought and behaviour" (*Ibid.*, p. 52). In Baudrillard's view, states Kellner, "In this post-modern world, individuals flee from the "desert of the real" for the ecstasics of hyperreality and the new realm of computer, media, and technological experience. In this universe, subjectivities are fragmented and lost, and a new terrain of experience appears that for Baudrillard rendered previous social theories and politics obsolete and irrelevant (*Ibid.*, p. 52).

For Baudrillard the world is now, more post-modern in nature as they are after hyperreality. According to Richard J. Lane, "In his account of the Vietnam war and *Apocalypse now*, Baudrillard is articulating a post-modern process whereby the "grand narratives" of progress technology and rationalism are replaced by the hyperreal world of third-order simulation: an excessive world of expenditure and psychedelic spectacle" (*Jean Baudrillard*, London: Routledge, 2007; p. 94). For Baudrillard, the first simulation would be where the representation of the real (e.g. a novel or a painting). It is artificial. The second order simulation blurs the boundaries between reality and representation (e.g. a map was drawn which exactly pictured the territory. The map has become as real as the real). The third order of simulation is hyperreality, which is a detachment from reality and representation (*Ibid.*, p. 86).

Baudrillard also claims that he is a nihilist. Nihilists reject authority, institutions, systems of belief and values. Friedrich Nietzsche was a nihilist. Post-modernism, for Baudrillard, is a play of "appearances". He also argues that in post-modern world we are involved in the empty and meaningless play of media (as in the pre-recorded piece of information, music or software). He calls the play of the media a "transparency" because all values become ultimately "indifferent forms' (*ibid.*, pp. 125-126).

(E) Frederic Jameson

According to Sean Homer, "post-modern theory has consistently have seen to challenge and undermine the central tenets of Marxist thought, especially the centrality it accords to class struggle as the driving force of history, the need for an analysis of the social as a "totality", and the primacy of the economic over political and cultural concerns" (Frederic Jameson" *post-modernism: The key figures*, edited by Hans Bertens and Joseph Natoli, Massachesetes. Blackwell Publishers, 2002. p180) Jameson did not reject the post-modern culture, but he looked forward a genuinely historical and dialectical analysis of its emergence and conditions of possibility (*Ibid.*, p. 181).

Jameson is an American Marxist thinker. His main writings are 'The cultural Turn' and 'post-modernism' or the cultural logic of Late Capitalism'. He sees a periodizing concept in post-modernism which serves to 'correlate the emergence of new formal features in culture with the emergence of a new type of social life and new economic order'(*Ibid.*, p. 183). Jameson is to 'always historicize'. Jameson sees the post-modern elements such as 'play' and 'indeterminacy' as form of deconstruction. According to Adam Roberts,' Jameson thinks he is actually talking about the techniques of deconstruction'. *(Frederic Jameson*, London: Routledge, 2007, p. 115).

(F) Richard Rorty (1931-)

He is an American philosopher. Post-modernism is for him uncompromisingly anti-respresentionalism anti-foundationalism, and anti-universalism. He was trying to bridge the gap between diverse philosophical traditions and schools, states Frans Ruiter "(Richard Rorty", *Post-modernism. The key figures, op cit*, p. 250). He appreciates rationalist philosophy and existential philosophy. He also appreciates enlightement philosopher Habermas and deconstructivist Derrida (*Ibid.*, p. 280).

His main works are 'The Linguistic Turn' and 'Philosophy and the Mirror of Nature'. According to Frans Ruiter, 'A curious aspect of Rorty's philosophy is that he would seem to represent a radical variety of post-modernism (anti-representationalism, anti-foundationalism, anti-universalism, anti-rationalism, historical contextualism, nominalism and so on)' (*Ibid.*, p. 283). He was critical of liberalism, which he understands the ideals of it as parochial, recent and eccentric developments (*Ibid.*, p. 284).

Rorty abandons the idea that mind is the mirror of nature. He proposes a new pragmatism which has the perspective that truth is non-realist, non essentialist (it has relation with other things) and non-representationalist. He is nominalist as he thinks that words have no intrinsic meaning, but only convention. He did not accept the modern view of self. He is also anti-foundationist (anti-foundationalism goes against the universal set of rules of rationality). He is also an advocate of cultural pluralism.

(G) Paul De Man

One of De Man's books is 'Blindness and insight: Essay in the Rhetoric contemporary criticism'. De man is a post structuralist. He is famous for Deconstructive literary criticism. According to Odell Scott, "De Man maintained that the purpose of deconstructive reading is to so respect the text, to read the text so closely, that those places where the text does not make sense to the reader become the very sites in need of elucidation, not in order to master the text, but in order to respect the self-decomposing of the text evident in such aporetic deadlocks, the very places where the text appears to contest or subvert its own stated intent or thesis" (David W. Odell-Scott, "Deconstruction" *Handbook of Post-modern Biblical interpretation*, p. 56.

It is noted by Spivak that, De Man's reading emphasized how the meaning of a text is not stable or transparent, but is radically indeterminate and therefore always open to further questioning. For De Man, the practice of literary criticism is not a matter of formulating a single, correct interpretation. He argues that texts contain blindspots which always and necessarily leads to errors and misreadings (*Gayatri Chakravorthy Spivak,* by Stephen Morton, p. 4). Drawing from De Man, Spivak states that the basis of truth claims no more than a trope. She also states that reading involves double movement in De Man. They are: (1) discovery that something that claims to be true is a mere trope (figurative or metaphorical),(2) how the corrective impulse within a tropological analysis is obliged to act out a lie in attempting to establish it as the corrected version of the truth (*Ibid.*, pp. 113-114). De Man argues that the rhetorical character of all language (whether philosophical or literary) opens up the possibility of misunderstanding (*Ibid.*, p. 114).

According to Paul De Man, "The structure of the text is not one of question and answer, but of a question whose meaning, is effaced from the moment it is asked" (Paul De Man,' Shelly Disfigured', *Deconstruction and Criticism*, New York, Continuum, 1999. p. 44).

B. Post-Colonial Philosophy

Post-colonial philosophy affirms the end of colonialism which subjugates, exploits and oppresses the colonized countries by the western powers. Post-colonialism views a world or a country which is free politically and economically. The Post-colonial era is a radical departure from the hegemonic powers. Post-colonial life is one of independent and liberated. The aggressive imperial powers have regulated once the life of the colonized, and colonizers have imposed their 'superiority' and authority over the colonized. The western powers have used not only political power, but also used all subtle means to dominate the people of the colonies.

The colonial powers have questioned the value and importance of traditional or indigenous knowledge. They also rejected the potentiality of the native people. The colonial powers always claim that they have more intelligence than the colonized. They also claim that their theories, perspectives and arguements are superior than the natives. The colonial powers have also claimed racial superiority. They also think that their view of life and habits are better than the colonized people. The colonial powers also have the perspective that their religious beliefs and practices are superior. These claims and perspectives of the colonial powers are being radically challenged by post-colonialism.

Hybridity is an important subject in post-colonialism. In McLeod's words, the subject becomes produced from the process of hybridisation. A person's subjectivity is composed from various sources, different materials, many locations-demolishing forever the idea of subjectivity as stable, single or 'pure' (John Mcleod, Beginning post-colonialism, New Delhi: Viva Books, 2010. p. 219). It is also stated that 'The concept of hybridity has proved very important for diaspora peoples, and indeed many others too, as a way of thinking beyond exclusionary, fixed, binary notions of identity based on ideas of rootedness and cultural, racial and national purity. Hybrid identities are never total and complete in themselves, like ordinary pathways but from crazy-paving. Instead, they remain perpetually in motion, pursuing errant and unpredictable routes, open to change and reinscription (*Ibid.*, p. 219). In hybridity 'new ethnicities' and new identities can be created. Multi-culturalism and multi-ethnicity are related to this hybridity. Cultural diversity and pluralism are (*Ibid.*, p. 225) part of hybridity (*Ibid.*, p. 227). It also creates a transnational forms of community (*Ibid.*, p. 231).

Post-colonial philosophy affirms the value of indigenous religion, culture, wisdom and way of life. It also upholds the identity and dignity of native people. Colonial philosophy is to subjugate, to rule over and even to annihilate the indigenous people. Post-colonialism draws our attention to the insensible and inhuman approach which is found in colonial philosophy. The colonial philosophy was to annihilate native people to control them or mix with them (by illicit sexual contact or by marriage). The last method was widely applied in certain countries by which there is a confusion about the new race. By using this method, the colonizers bring confusion over the native people. By this means the identity of native people became a confused identity. Philosophy is a view of life. The colonial philosophy is to use all deceptive means to dominate the colonized people and to tap their energy and resources, and to enslave them. This spirit of domineering is challenged by post-colonialism. Post-colonial philosophy affirms what is native or indigenous and contextual and it is liberative. Post-colonialism promotes nationalism and nation-building.

2. The Key Post-Colonial Thinkers

(A) Edward Said

His famous book is 'Orientalism'. He is understood as an originator of colonial discourse theory. Post-colonialism deals with impact of European conquest on colonized societies. It deals with political struggle and cultural struggle. There is an impact of language also on colonised societies. One of the examples from the ancient past is the hellenization of Greeks. English, Latin and Spanish languages are imposed on colonized countries by the western countries.

Edward Said talks about the worldliness of the text as text is located in the world. For Said, 'a text, in its actually being a text, is being in the world', states Bill Ashcroft and Paul Ahluwalia (*Edward Said*, London: Reutledge, 2007. p. 21). In Said's opinion, texts announce their materality, their worldliness by their situatedness in just the same way as speech (*Ibid.*, p. 22). In the post-colonial societies, there is dominance of colonial languages. In most of the colonial societies, they are speaking some one's language and not theirs. Said states, the languages in which we are speaking is his before it is mine'. Looking at the possibilities of critical reading, Edward Said suggests 'affiliation' which is a process of identification through culture which is closer to worldliness of text, than filiation which refers to lines of descent in nature or heritage. For him, states Ashcroft and Ahlualia, 'an affiliative reading allows the critic to see the literary work as a phenomenon in the world, located in a network of non-literary, non-canonical and non-traditional affiliations' (*Ibid.*, p 25).

Affiliation is understood as a feature of text's worldliness. Affiliation enables the text to maintain itself as a text, the status of the author, historical moment, conditions of publication, diffusion and reception, values drawn upon and values and ideas assumed. Affiliation draws us to the location and locatednsess of the text's production (*Ibid.*, pp. 25-26). According to Ashcroft and Ahluwalia, "For Edward said the world from which the text originated, the world with which it was affiliated, was crucial, not only for the business of interpretation but also for its ability to make an impact on readers". (*Ibid.*, p. 27).

According to Ashcroft and Ahluwalia, "Orientalism, in Said's formulation, is principally a way of defining and 'locating' Europe's others. But as a group of related disciplines, orientalism was, in important ways, about Europe itself, and hinged on arguments that circulated around the issue of national distinctiveness, and racial and linguistic origins'(*Ibid.*, pp. 50-51). The word orient refers to the colonies, for the British and the French. But for

Americans, it refers to far East, especially Japan and China (*Ibid.*, p. 57). His one way of defining orientalism as a corporate institution is demonstrative of its amorphous capacity as a structure used to dominate and authorise the orient. This view is linked to colonialism (*Ibid.*, p. 57). According to Edward Said, the power of the orientalists lay in their 'knowing' the orient, which in itself constituted power and yet also was an exercise in power (*Ibid.*, p. 68).

While summarizing Edward Said's understanding on 'orientalism', Ashcroft and Ahluwalia stated, "the essence of Said's argument is that to know something is to have power over it and conversely, to have power is to be able to know the world in your own terms. When this something is a whole region of the world in which dozens of ethnicities, nationalities and languages are gathered under the spurious category the orient, then the link between that knowledge and the power it confirms becomes profoundly important" (*Ibid.*, p. 83).

In Edward Said's book 'culture and imperialism', he talks about the imperial culture which justify and reinforce the establishment and exploitation of empire, and the other is countering this idea, that is the historical experience of resistance against empire (*Ibid.*, p. 87). Imperial culture is the most powerful instrument of imperial hegemony (*Ibid.*, p. 88). For Said, imperialism is the practice, theory, and attitude of dominating metropolitan centre ruling a distant territory. Colonalism, for him, is implanting of settlements on a distant territory (*Ibid.*, p. 90). In order to understand the imperial presence in text, Said suggest the contrapuntal reading. It is explained as a form of 'reading back' from the perspective of the colonised, to show how the submerged but crucial presence of the empire emerges in canonical texts. As we begin to read, not univocally but contrapuntally, with a simultaneous awareness of both of the metropolitan history and other subjected and concealed histories against which the dominant discourse acts and we obtain a different sense of what is going on in the text (*Ibid.*, p. 92).

According to Ashcroft and Ahluwalia, "Contrapuntal reading is a technique of theme and variation by which a counterpoint is established between the imperial narrative and the post-colonial perspective, a 'counter-narrative, that keeps penetrating beneath the surface of the individual texts to elaborate the ubiquitous presence of imperialism in canonical culture" (*Ibid.*, p. 93). The both dimensions of polyphony is considered by contrapuntal reading. Said talks about two phases of decolonisation: (1) recovery of geographical territory, (2) 'Changing of cultural territory'. The primary resistance involves fighting against outside intrusion, and the secondary resistance entails ideological or cultural reconstitution. For Said, resistance is a process in the rediscovery and repatriation of what had been suppressed in the natives' past by the process of imperialism (*Ibid.*, p. 108). Said describes negritude as a nativist phenomenon which linked with anti-colonial stances (*Ibid.*, p. 110).

(B) Gayatri Chakravorty Spivak (1942-)

It is observed, "Gayatri Chakravorty Spivak is best known for her overtly political use of contemporary cultural and critical theories to challenge the legacy of colonialism on the way we read and think about literature and culture. What is more, Spivak's critical interventions encompass a range of theoretical interests, including Marxism, Feminism, deconstruction, post-colonial theory and cutting-edge work on globalisation" (Stephen Morton, *Gayatri Chakravorty Spivak*, London: Routledge: 2007. p.) Gayatri Spivak was born in Calcutta (India), and did her early education in India. She had her higher education in the West. Her works include, 'The post-colonial critic' and 'A critique of post-colonial reason'. According to Stephen Morton, Spivak has foregrounded the textual elements that shape our understanding of the social world and where by questioned the binary opposition between philosophical or literary texts and the socalled real world (*Ibid.*; p. 4) In the words of Morton, 'Spivak exposes how the world is represented from the dominant perspective and geopolitical location of the 'First world' to the exclusion of other disenfranchised groups' (*Ibid.*, p. 5). She was critical of the historian of subaltern studies who used Marxian methodology. She was emphasizing, Morton states, that western Marxist model of social change that these historians employ does not do justice to the complex histories of subaltern insurgency and resistance that they seek to recover (*Ibid.*, p. 7). She had opinion that the complex life of third world women cannot be properly represented by the vocabulary of western critical theory (*Ibid.*, p. 7).

Spivak was anxious about the fact that Indian nationalism has failed to emancipate the lower class, subaltern women. According to Morton the argument of Spivak is that before we can learn anything about the economic text of globalisation or the patriarchal oppression of 'Third World' women, we must first unlearn the privileged system of western knowledge that have indirectly served the interests of colonialism and neo-colonialism (*Ibid.*, p. 9). Talking about the development of World Bank and World Trade Organization, Spivak refers that this dominant representation of the world as 'worlding', or the assumption that when the colonizers came to the world, they encounter it as uninscribed earth upon which they write their inscriptions (*Ibid.*, p. 18). According to Morton, "the term 'worlding in Spivak's work refers to the way in which writing in general, or textuality, has provided a rhetorical structure to justify imperial expansion" (*Ibid.*, p. 19). It is stated by Morton that at time Spivak uses the term epistemic violence to emphasize how western knowledge or epistemology has been used to justify the violent exercise of political and military force over other non-western cultures (*Ibid.*, p. 19). Spivak was referred by Colin Mac Cabe as a 'Feminist Marxist deconstructivist' According to Morton, "For Spivak, the 'political' value of a deconstructive reading practice is that it guards against the universal claims of Marxism, national liberation movements or western feminism to speak for all the oppressed" (*Ibid.*, p. 35).

Spivak was critical of the western feminists for ignoring the specific experiences of 'Third World' women when they construct a universal feminist subject, states Morton (*Ibid.*, p. 40). In Spivak one can see the influence of Derrida's deconstruction in the development of post-colonial thought. In the words of Stephen Morton, the experience of disempowered, subaltern groups in the post-colonial world present an ethical dilemma as well as a methodological challenge to Spivak. Her writings also demonstrate the experience of social and political oppression in post-colonial societies such as India cuts across differences in class, region, language, ethnicity, religion, generation, gender and citizenship (*Ibid.*, p. 46). Spivak, states Morton, emphasizes that the classical Marxist methodology of the subaltern studies collective prevents them from reading the histories of women's resistance in India (*Ibid.*, p. 47). Spivak also has the opinion that the subaltern women are silenced by British colonization and the Hindu patriarchal spirit (*Ibid.*, p. 64).

One of Spivaks contribution, states Morton, is that she demands that feminism should consider seriously the material histories and lives of 'Third World' women in its account of women's struggle against oppression (*Ibid.*, p. 71). In her view on subaltern women, she challenges the universal claims of feminism to speak for all women (*Ibid.*, p. 71). For her, it is not adequate to speak for all women as western feminists do regardless of cultural difference, states Morton (*Ibid.*, p. 78). Spivak challenges the universal humanist assumption that all women's lives and histories are the same. She also stresses the importance of global political awareness of the local Economic, Political, Social and Cultural conditions that structure women's oppressions in different parts of the world (*Ibid.*, p. 91).

According to Stephen Morton, 'Spivak's engagement

with post-colonial texts is motivated in part by a desire to challenge the totalizing system of subaltern agency or resistance' (*Ibid.*, p. 123). She is also critical of the political promises of Third World nationalism and decolonisation, especially from the perspective of subaltern women and the underclass (*Ibid.*, p. 124). She was quite aware of the domineering elements in nationalism. She argues, states Morton, that post-colonial nationalism is divided between the state political programmes of ruling governmental elites and the popular struggles of the people who are often ignored by the dominant political programmes (*Ibid.*, p. 124). For her, if history is written from the perspective of the struggles of the marginated (e.g.; popular struggles and peasant rebellions) that literature can provide a rhetorical space for subalterns to re-articulate the suppressed histories of people's struggles (*Ibid.*, p. 124). Spivak was suggesting an ethics of reading which is more sensitive to the location of subaltern women, says Morton. She argues for the notion of ethics as a responsibility of the self (western) to the other (non-western).

Gayatri Chakravorty Spivak was known as a post-colonial critic, and she was very cautious of the nationalism and post-colonial thinking which fail to consider the situation and the struggles of the subaltern. She was very much influenced by post-modern thinking, especially of the Deconstruction of Derrida.

(C) Homi K. Bhabha (1949-)

He was born in a Parsi community in Bombay. At present he is teaching English and American literature at Harvard

University. He provides a working theory of cultural hybridity. For him, the new internationalism is a history of post-colonial migration, the narratives of cultural and political diaspora and the major social displacements of peasants and aboriginal communities (*The Location of Culture*, London: Routledge Classics, 1994. p. 7). So Bhabha states that the concepts such as homogeneous national cultures, consensual transmission of historical traditions or 'organic' ethnic communities are in need of redefenition (*Ibid.*, p. 7). He also states, "Post-coloniality, for its part, is a salutary reminder of the persistent 'neo-colonial' relations within the 'new' world order and the multinational division of labour. Such a perspective enables the authentication of histories of exploitation and the evolution of strategies of resistance" (*Ibid.*, p. 9).

Bhabha explains the 'hybridity' as follows: "Private and Public, post and present, the psyche and the social develop an interstitial intimacy. It is an intimacy that questions binary divisions through which such spheres of social experiences are often spatially opposed. These spheres of life are linked though an 'in-between' temporality that takes the measure of dwelling at home, while producing an image of the world of history. This is the moment of aesthetic distance that provides the narrative with a double edge, which like the coloured south African subject represents a hybridity, a difference 'within', a subject that inhabits the rim of an 'in-between' reality (*Ibid.*, p. 9). The south African coloured is affected by displacement, exile or diaspora and living in ghettoes which are 'unhomely' situations.

Bhabha talks also about the importance of hybrid

moment of political change. He argues for the negotiation between gender and class. For him, the transformational value of change lies in the rearticulation, or translation, of elements that are *neither the one* unitary working class, *nor the other* (the pòlitics of gender) *but something else besides* which contests the terms and territories of both (*Ibid.*, p. 41). Hybridity, for him is not unifying the elements, but to have negotiations with them. He argues along with Stuart Hall, the construction of a counter hegenomic power block which consists of unemployed, semi-skilled and unskilled, part-time workers, male and female, the low paid, black people, underclass. It is a structure of heterogeneity, signs of fragmentation of class and cultural consensus which is related to historical experience of contemporary social division. This kind of hybridity is used as a political alternative. It can be also called the principle of political negotiation (*Ibid.*, p. 41).

Entering into the 'Third space' is the context of international culture or diversity of cultures where, Bhabha says, the articulation of culture's hybridity (*Ibid.*, p. 56). According to him, this third space has a colonial or post-colonial provenance. Bhabha states, 'we should remember that it is the 'inter'—The cutting edge of translation and negotiation, the *in-between* space—that carries the burden of the meaning of culture. It makes it possible to begin envisaging national, anti-nationalist histories of the, 'people'. And by exploring this Third space, we may elude the politics of polarity and emerge on the others of ourselves' (*Ibid.*, p. 56).

The indigenous traditions engage in post-colonial

struggle against the dominant relations of power and knowledge states Bhabha. It may sound that Bhabha's view of hybridity is a post-colonial discussion in his own way, and not strictly anti-colonial and anti-hegemonic. His approach takes a middle position to integrate the opposites which is found in politics in the form of negotiations. It is also to be noted that some of the socalled prominent post-colonial thinkers live in the west and formed post-colonial theories, philosophies and theologies using the western resources theories and methods, which are not quite suiting to the third world situation (i.e., the victimized or marginated people and their struggles). A radical departure from the colonial/hegemonic powers is inevitable. A movement towards indigeneity (appreciation of what is native), contextuality and liberative spirit is essential for post-colonial approach. And post-colonialism should not be a space for any kind of arbitrary discussions.

Bhabha was concerned of the site of culture which is temporal. According to him, cultural differences must not be understood as the free play of polarities in the homogeneous empty time of the national community, but it is the jarring of meanings and values generated in the process of cultural interpretation as an effect of the preplexity of living in the liminal spaces of national society (*Ibid.*, p. 232).

IV

The Post-Modern and Post-Colonial Hermeneutics

Before entering into the post-modern and post-colonial interpretations, it is important to discuss some of the current thinking in relation to hermeneutics. Selected prominent thinking and thinkers in hermeneutics are discussed over here.

(A) Structuralism

An important structuralist is Claude Levi-Strauss, who was (b. 1908) from France. He tried to build connections between anthropology and linguistics. He was a structural anthopologist. Structuralism is rooted in the semiology of the Swiss linguist Ferdinant de Saussure. Structuaralism sees things objectively and corporately. It includes the system analysis. The background of structuralism is linguistics and cultural anthropology. Ferdinant de Saussure (1857-1913) was a scholar in linguistics. According to him, language is not a personal or individual phenomenon, but it is rooted in the mutual structural relationship of humanity. So the structural analysis of literature (in poetics and literary criticism) was developed. The signifying and signified, gestures, religious rituals, practices, concepts, meanings are all part of the structure of language, because these factors communicate.

Structuralists do not give importance to author. They take literature as a discourse, and meaning is related to the existence of structure. It is not only questioning the centrality of the author, but also the audience in interpretation. The connections of the text to the author who intended it and to a reader who interprets it are excluded by structuralism. Structuralism is an attempt to extend to semantics (study of meaning) and to all semiological (study of symbols) disciplines which are related to phonology (sound). For structuralism, language is an object and that can be investigated scientifically.

De Saussure studied code or the set of codes which form the structure of the system of various languages than historical roots and evolution of languages. For him, language is not a *substance* but *form*. It treats collection of signs as a closed system and autonomous system of internal dependencies. He made distinction between language as *langue* and *parole*. Langue refers to code or lexical systems and units such as phonemes, lexemes, morphemes and syntagma. Parole refers to language as the activity of speaking subjects who intend to say something to someone about something. The core unit studied by structuralism is sign or sign system. Structural linguists after Saussure, states Graham Alen, studies the language system, the roles and codes rather than studying the speech, actual acts of language (parole) (*Roland Barthes*, London: Routlege, 2007.

p. 40). The parole or acts of language is possible because of language system.

Structuralism makes distinction between state of the systems (synchrony) and science of changes (diachrony) and subordinates latter to the former. It studies the differences and oppositions of the signs within the system of language as at a given moment and leaves aside any consideration of the process of change of meaning in language.

The work of De Saussure was 'Course on General Linguistics'. According to Graham Alen, Saussure imagine a science that would be able to read systematically all human sign system. His linguistic theories revolutionalized the approach to language, formerly dominated by philology, that is study the history of words (*Roland Barthes*, London: Routledge, 2007: p. 39). A sign, for De Saussure, is the culmination of a material signifier (sound or written mark) and a signified (concept). The signified is not the object or action but mental concept (*Ibid.*, p. 40). Sign means signifier and signified. For example, 'red light' is the signifier, and signified is 'stop the car'.

Roland Barthes (1915-980) is a French literary critic and structualist. His main works were 'mythologies', 'writing degree zero' and 'Elements of semiology'. One would find structuralist and post-structuralist elements is Barthes. He was influenced by Swiss linguist Ferdinant de Saussure. He was interested in structuralism and semiology or semiotics. Semiology is the science of signs. When Barthes refer structure, states Graham Alen, he is referring to the idea of a system (language) out of which utterances (Parole) are generated (*Ibid.*, p. 40). Structuralism is found in major disciplines of the Humanities and social sciences: literary study, sociology, history, anthropology, psycho-analysis, philosophy and linguistics (*Ibid.*, p. 41). In Barthes, semiology is referring to study on sign systems, but structuralism is employed in his analysis of literary narratives (*Ibid.*, p. 41). Sign, for him, is the relationship between signifier and a signified. For Barthes, myth is a peculiar system, in that it is constructed from a semiological chain which existed before it (*Ibid.*, p. 43). Myth transforms first order meanings into second-order meanings. Myth hijacks meaning and turns it into a second order meaning or what Barthes calls signification. Myth is a meta-language (*Ibid.*, p. 44). Myth is a meta-language means a second order language which acts on a first-order language, a language which generates meaning out of already existent meaning (*Ibid.*, p. 44). The photograph of a French black soldier can be mythically referring about French nation. But if we understand only as a single individual, it goes back to the first order of literal meaning.

For Barthes, the structural analyst should disregard parole. A scientific approach to analysis of narrative must change from inductive approach (extrapolating meaning from a individual examples) to deductive approach (establishing a working model against which to test all individual examples). He argues for structural analysis of narratives as a model. Linguistics, Barthes states, stops at the sentence. Narratives, he argues, contain many sentences (larger than sentence). Narratives are discourses which are understood as the broader categories of linguistic representation in the society (*Ibid.*, p. 56).

The narrative, for Barthes, has three levels. The basic level of primary units is called *functions*. The next higher level is called *Actions*, and the final level is called *Narrative* itself. Functions include all elements of narrative as everything has meaning in narrative text (e.g.; telephone ringing). Action represents the character in the narratives. Character may be evil or good, represented by their talk, walk and dress (*Ibid.*, p. 59). Narrative comes from the system of narratives and its meaning is always mediated (that which passes through a process or system of transformation in its representation) (*Ibid.*, p. 60).

A shift of thinking is found in Roland Barthes as an influence of Derrida's post-structrualist thought. Barthes essay 'The Death of the Author' situate him as a post-structralist. This essay is noted for his betrayal of structuralism. This essay is a transitional one. It indicates his movement from structuralism to post-structuralism. He did become concerned of textuality, intertextuality, the plurality and the infinite play of meaning within literary and other kinds of work (*Ibid.*, p. 74).

(B) Post-Structuralism

The post-modern thinkers like Derrida and Foucault are post-structuralists. Foucault was not interested in author, text and implications. For Derrida, author is not important. The inquiry for fixed and present meaning is not useful in Derrida's perspective. There is no fixed meaning for any symbols. It challenges the structuralism. Deconstruction is not destruction of structure, but showing how text itself is found deconstructed. Deconstruction is a reading in which new texts are created in repeated reading. Derrida rejects the essence of symbols, so it is an atheism in linguistics. The writing may go against the author, so the death of the author.

Giles Deleuze (1925-95) is known as a French intellectual whose thoughts are post-structural in character. According to Clare Colebrook, "post-structuralism responded to the impossibility of founding knowledge either on pure experience (phenomenology) or systematic structures (structuralism)" (*Giles Deleuze*, London: Routledge, 2007. p. 2). Deleuze was trying to re-read the philosophy. He had studies on philosophers like Hume, Nietzsche, Bergson, Kant, Spinoza, Foucault and Leibniz. His works include 'Difference and Repetition' and 'The logic of sense'. According to Colebrook, "Post-structuralism sought to explain the emergence, becoming or genesis of structures: how systems such as language both come into being and how they mutate through time. For this reason, Deleuze and those of his generation sought to conceptualise both difference and becoming, but a difference and becoming that would not be the becoming of something. Their main target was not just the recent movements of phenomenology and structuralism, but the entire history of western thought" (*Ibid.*, p. 3). Hegel argued that consciousness or spirit could overcome all difference and becoming, as he understood that the becoming and difference of life and history could be comprehended within one single moment of spirit. For post-structuralists, Hegel (G.W.F. Hegel, the German Philosopher, 1770-1831) was an advocate of the western suppression of difference (*Ibid.*, p. 3).

According to Colebrook, 'post-structuralists looked at the opening, excess or instability of systems: the way languages, organisms, cultures, and political systems mutate or *become*' (*Ibid.*, p. 3). The difference and becoming are central to Deleuze's approach. Deleuze proposes a 'transcendental empiricism', which insists that there is no grounds, subject or being who experiences, just experience. The cosmos is understood as a 'phenomenon' of intersecting flows of life, all propelled by difference (*Ibid.*, p. 87). Life is understood as a virtual multiplicity.

Deleuze's 'transcendental empiricism' is based on the challenge of life, states Colebrook. He also opines that Deleuze's method thinks of experience well beyond its human and fixed images. This is understood as an ethical and practical task. It frees us from the restrictions of common sense and moral image of human reason, allowing us to become towards the future (Ibid., p. 89). Deleuze argues that, there becomings, such as action, perceptions, variation, and from this flux of becomings we perceive or organize beings. He also insists that we value actions and becoming itself, freed from any human norm or end (goal). Becoming in Deleuze is a radical concept which goes beyond ordinary perceptions of life, but a new perception (*Ibid.*, p. 145).

Another most important figure in post-structuralism is Julia Kristeva (b. 1941). She was born in Bulgeria. Kristeva and others in her circle looked for dynamic and changing aspects of systems. Post-structuralism looked at systems diachronically. She claimed that she was one of the people who helped to formulate a type of post-structuralism (Noelle McAfee, *Julia Kristeva*, London: Routledge, 2007. pp. 6-7). Kristeva thought that it is essential to 'dynamize' the structure by taking into consideration the speaking subject and its unconscious experience on the one hand and, on the other the pressures of other social structures (*Ibid.*, p 7).

Her main books are 'Semiotics: Investigations for Semanalysis' 'Nations without Nationalism' and 'Revolution in poetic language'. Her fictions include 'The Samirai', The old man and the wolve's and the detective novel 'possessions'. She is a practising psychoanalyst. In the book 'Revolution in poetic language' she wrote that our philosophies of language, embodiments of the idea, are nothing more than the thoughts of archivists, archaeologists and necrophiliacs. According to McAfee, this means that most non-post-structuralist theories of language treat language as a dead artifact, something that can be catalouged, achieved, entombed—a formal object of study. It denies the dynamic processes in which people generate meaning and experience (*Ibid.*, p. 14). Kristeva, according to McAfee tries to see language as a signifying process rather than separate, and static entity (*Ibid.*, p. 14). The theory of signifying process in Kristeva has two modes—the semiotic and symbolic. Semiotic is the extraverbal way in which bodily energy and affects make their way into language. The symbolic includes both the subject's drive and articulations. The symbolic is a way of signifying that depends on language as a sign system complete with its grammar and syntax, states Kristeva (*Ibid.*, p. 17). The symbolic is a mode of signifying in which speaking beings attempt to express meaning with as little ambiguity as possible. The expressions of scientists and logicians are paradigmatic example of people trying to use symbolic language, whereas expression found in music, dance and poetry exemplify the semiotic. The semiotic could not be seen as the mode of expression that originate in the unconscious whereas the symbolic could be seen as the conscious way a person tries to express using a stable sign system (whether, written, spoken or gestured with sign language). Both these elements are important in Kristeva's perspective, states McAfee (*Ibid.*, p. 17).

It is stated that before the subject begins to use language symbolically—through the use of symbols, grammar and syntax—there are expressions through intonations and gestures (e.g. baby's cooes and babbles or the imitations of the rhythm of parents speech). This kind of signifying is what, according to McAfee, Kristeva calls semiotic. Kristeva uses the term 'chora' along with semiotics, so semiotic chora. Chora can refer to unnamable, hybrid or improbable. It is related to intonations, rhythms or gestures of a child who does not yet know how to use language to refer to objects (*Ibid.*, p. 19). Kristeva also talks about Genotext and Phenotext which roughly refers the distinction between semiotic and symbolic. The term semanalysis is used by Kristeva to denote the discourse of semiotic analysis. Intertextuality is used to refer by her as 'passage from one sign system to another'. It is a transposition of one sign system to another. It also accepts the plurality and polysemy (the multiple levels or kinds of meaning).

Kristeva was concerned of women. She is of the opinion that difference of what is masculine and feminine cannot be escaped. Kristeva, states McAfee, likes sexual difference, but she wants this difference to be one that is neither masochistic nor constraining, but productive and freeing for women and their sexuality (*Ibid.*, p. 103). She states that it is not just men and patriarchy are guilty of oppressing women but all people are equally guilty. It also stresses the fact that there are many rivalries within us (*Ibid.*, p. 102). She also exposes the need of a culture of revolt, without which our psyche is in danger of withering away. Speaking being, for her, need to revolt against the culture of the show, against rigid symbolic structures and against homogeneous identities, in order to create and maintain a psychic space or inner zone (*Ibid.*, p. 118).

(C) Philosophical Hermeneutics

Some of the important figures of Philosophical Hermeneutics are considered in this section.

(I) Martin Heidegger (1889-1977)

He was German existentialist philosopher. His master piece is 'Being and time'. He used hermeneutics to have a longer quest for fundamental ontology. He sought a method of going behind the root of western conceptions of Being. He deals with 'that which shows itself, the manifested, the revealed'. According to him, ontology should turn to the process of understanding and interpretation through which things appear. The primary task of interpretation is to bring things from hiddenness or concealment. Philosophically, he said, hermeneutics sets forth the basic structures of possibility of 'Dasein'.

In his hermeneutics, the word understanding is important. It is suggesting sympathy, and the capacity to feel something of what another person is experiencing. It is participating in the thing understood, not merely objective knowledge. Understanding is the power to grasp one's own possibilities for being, within the context of the life-world in which one exists. Understanding is the basis for all interpretation. The essence of understanding lies not in simply grasping one's situation but in the disclosure of concrete possibilities for being within the horizons of one's placement in the world. According to Heidegger, understanding operates within the 'hermeneutical circles', that is the interpreted relationships. In his view, the 'world' is very significant. It is the personal world is what he meant. We should, he states, conceive the world not as separate from the self. There are something which are unclear in the world. It is important to find out meaning of objects that is, to find out the intention.

Heidegger uses the word 'meaningfulness' to designate the ontological ground for the intelligibility of the fabric of relationships and it is the basis for language. Interpretation, he says, is simply the rendering explicit of understanding. Language is the house of being, and it must be interpreted. According to him, interpretation is never a presupposition less grasping of something given in advance. He argues that the text should be approached questioningly, not with blank openness. His analysis weds hermeneutics to existential ontology and to phenomenology, and it point to a ground for hermeneutics not in subjectivity but in the facticity of world in the historicality of understanding. (*Hermeneutics* by Richard E Palmer, Evanston: South Western University Press, 1969. pp. 126-293).

(II) Hans-Georg Gadamer (1900-2002)

Gadamer's famous book is 'Truth and Method'. His hermeneutical method is dialectical, the dialectics between understanding (Truth) and explanation (method). Experience is important, according to him, where knowing is simply a stream of perceptions but a happening, an event, an encounter. Experience, according to him, has its dialectical fulfilment not in a knowing but in an openness for experience. Experience is non-objecitfiable accumulation of understanding or wisdom. Experiences, for him, is the new understanding which is constantly acquired. True experience, in his view, is experience of one's own historicality. Unless there is right question there is no right answer. We find the right question through the immersion in the subject itself. According to him, authentic interpretation will relate itself to the question placed by the text. (The text has a place and a subject). The first thing, in his view, is to understand the horizon of meaning or of questioning within which the direction of the meaning of the text is determined. He opined that man has a world; and language discloses one's world. Understanding, in his view, is historical, dialectical and linguistic event. According to Gadamer, the text must be allowed speak, the reader being open to it as a subject in its own right rather than as an object. The hermeneutical experience is an encounter between heritage in the form of a transmitted text and the horizon of the interpreter. It is the fusion of horizons in his perspective. Language is an open space and there is a common horizon possible because of our belongingness to language and because of the belongingness of the text to language. The emergence of common horizon is what fusion of Horizons for Gadamer. The interpreter is to see what is in the text as to follow and to participate in what is said by the text. The interpretation of the text is not passive openness but dialectical interaction with the text. The task of hermeneutics is to take seriously the linguisticality of language and experiences to develop a truly historical hermeneutics.

Gadamer states that understanding involves something like applying the text to be understood to the interpreter's present situation (Anthony C. Thieselton, New Horizons in Hermeneutics, p. 220) Langauage is the medium of hermeneutical experience, for Gadamer. Thieselton states that Gadamer understands translation as interpretation, that is to put material into his or her own "world". It is to bring, the two horizons together. It can be referred in Gadamer's terms 'concretion of historically-effected consciousness'. It is the historicality of interpretation (*ibid*, p. 222).

According to Gadamer, understanding is always a historical, dialectical and linguistic event. The key to understanding is openness and participation. He was also influenced by Heidegger's view of understanding. Gadamer divided the hermeneutics into three spheres-aesthetic, historical and the sphere of language. (*Hermeneutics* by Richard E. Palmer, Evanston: North Western University Press, 1969, pp. 194-ff).

(III) Wilhelm Dilthey (1833-1911)

He was a German philosopher and historian. Dilthey stressed the uniqueness and particularity of individuals, as well as what they shared in common, and he also gave an important place to the creative power of human imagination. Key to his hermeneutical understanding is centred on life ('Leben') or 'Lived experience'. 'Life' represents the shared flow of human activities and experiences which together constitute human experience both in its social diversity and in its individual particularity. Dilthey says that what we grasp through experience and understanding is life as the interweaving of all mankind. So understanding of other people and their expressions is developed on the basis of experience and self understanding and the constant interaction between them. These expressions, in his view, include signs, symbols, speech, writings, practices and action.

In Dilthey's view, the task of the interpreter is to gain understanding of the other through re-living the other's experience by stepping into the other's shoes on the basis of empathy or transposition. He was aware that "I" differs from "other", but, for him, understanding is the re-discovery of the "I" in the "Thou". He understood a 'life-relation' between the self and the other. He emphasized 'life' and 'reconstruction'.

According to Joseph Putti, Dilthey is not concerned with what the text says but with what lies behind it. His aim is to gain an empathetic understanding of the individual behind the text who has expressed himself in the text. It is the life of another that is sought, not the meaning of the text of life.(*Theology as Hermeneutics*, p. 134).

Wilhelm Dilthey was attempting to make hermeneutics a basis for the human sciences or humannities states Thieselton (*Hermeneutics: An Introduction*, Michigam Willian Eerdmans Publishing Co., 2009. p. 161). Dilthey established life or lived experience as the key category of human being (*Ibid.*, p. 162). According to Thieselton, "life" is a shared flow of human activities and experiences, in both social diversity and the individuals experience (*Ibid.*, p. 162). These experiences for Dilthey are connected and are expressed in common language of signs, symbols, speech, writing and in human practices and in institution such as laws (*Ibid.*, p. 162). In Thieselton's opinion Dilthey has contributed three things to hermeneutics: (1) He extended hermeneutics to include law, social sciences and all human institutions beyond language. If it applies to language, hermeneutics applies to all human society and its concrete institutions (2) Dilthey insisted that both interpretation and objects of interpretation are radically conditioned by their place in history, or historicality. (3) Dilthey uses "life" as the common medium between objects of interpretation and the interpreter. The interpreter is to "relive" the other's experience by stepping out of his or her shoes and exercising "sympathy" or "transposition" (*Ibid.*, p. 163).

(IV) Emileo Betti

He was an Italian historian of law. Betti believes that hermeneutics as an intellectual discipline and educational training is fundamental for life. According to him, whether we are interpreting a historical text, or listening to a conversation, we need to reach behind the words themselves to see what is the main train of thought which gave rise to them. He states that imaginative reconstruction with the use of sympathy, and insight is required for understanding what has to be understood transcends the systematic meaning of text or utterance.

Understanding, he says, is reversal or inversion of the creative process in which the interpreter has to make his hermeneutical way back along with the creative path, carrying on the process of re-thinking. He sees self-understanding as the product not of introspection but of the flow of inter-subjective life and encounter.

He suggests four "moments" of hermeneutical process. They are as follows:

(a) Interpreter investigates the linguistic phenomena of the speech or text.
(b) In a critical 'moment' the interpreter sees to gain self-awareness of social interests, ideologies, commitments, or sources of intolerance that may hinder genuine openness to understand.

(c) He invites the interpreter to place himself in the shoes of the person to be understood, using imagination and insight.

(d) Reconstruction extends to the entire situation and set of conditions which work together to lead to the production of the utterance of the text.

Betti insists on the existential relationship between the interpreter and the object (Text). To the object (text) he developed two canons.

1. The canon of the hermeneutical autonomy of the object and immanence of the hermeneutical standard.
2. The canon of totality and coherence of hermeneutical evaluation and to the subject of interpretation. For this second canon also be developed two canons.
   (a) The canon of the actuality of understanding
   (b) The canon of the harmonization of understanding: hermeneutical correspondence and agreement (Josef Bleicher, The Hermeneutic Imagination, London: Routledge & Kegan Paul, 1982, p. 67).

(V) Paul Ricoeur (1913-2005)

He is a French Philosopher whose interests are existentialism, linguistic theory, psychoanalysis, structuralism, theories of texts, metaphor, theology and religions. He is the proponent of 'Hermeneutics of suspicion. In his view, to interpret is to understand a double meaning. A symbol, in his opinion, is a double meaning expression. He urges us to show willingness to listen and to suspect. He argues about 'levels' or 'layers' of meaning. He advocated for the 'surplus of meaning' of the text. According to him, symbols requires interpretation because it is a figure of double-meaning language and contains surplus of meaning or an overdetermination which releases itself to understanding only by way of interpretation of surplus, says Joseph Putti (*Theology as Hermeneutics*, p. 142).

According to Ricoeur, the meaning of what is said is important. The distanciation of the speaker from the text is essential as the subjectivity of the speaker is replaced by that of text. The text achieves semantic autonomy. What matters is that, the text means more than what the author meant when he wrote it. There is distanciation of the text from the original audience. The semantic autonomy of the text from the original readers open up the range of potential readers and creates the audience of text. What matters is the response of this audience. Ricoeur urges to consider three things in the text (Written text) the composition, the genre, and the style (*Theology as Hermeneutics*, p. 148).

In Ricoeur's view, the metaphors have surplus of meaning as they have the character of polysemy, more than one meaning. Hermeneutics is understood by him as a movement from understanding (Verstehen) to explanation (Erklaren) and explanation to comprehension. The ultimate aim of all hermeneutics, for him, is comprehension (*Ibid.*, pp. 149-156). To comprehend means to appropriate, that is to make ones own what was previously foreign (*Ibid.*, p. 156). According to Ricoeur, "Not the intention of the author, which is supposed to be hidden behind the text; not the historical situation common to the author and his original readers; not the expectations of feelings of these original historical and cultural phenomenon. What has to be appropriated is the meaning of the text itself, conceived in a dynamic way the direction of thought opened up by the text" *(Interpretation Theory; Discourse and the Surplus Meaning*, p. 92, quoted in *Theology as Hermeneutics*, p. 156). For Ricoeur, the hermeneutical task is not to re-discover the original author, or the reader or the context. In his view, the letters of St. Paul are no less addressed to us than to the Romans and Galatians. The meaning of a text is open to anyone who can read. This universality (guaranteed by the omni-temporality of meaning) alone generates new speech events (*Ibid.*, p. 156).

In Ricoeur's perspective, each symbol has threefold dimension—cosmic, oneiric and poetic. If evil is taken as an example, the cosmic dimension as an evil force (cosmic) and the cosmic aspect is experienced subjectively in a psychic response, e.g. fear or dread (oneiric) and then symbol is emerged into language in the form of word or ritual (poetic)-(*Theology as Hermeneutics*, pp. 108 109). Ricoeur favoured a creative interpretation of symbol. For him, "symbols give rise to thought". The explanation is understood by him as the willingness to expose and to abolish dols which are projections of human will. Understanding is the willingness to listen with openness to symbols. He argues for socio-critical suspicion and post-critical retrieval embodying openness towards new possibility which will bring change (Anthony C. Thieselton, *New Horizons in Hermeneutics*, p. 344). Ricoeur argues that the 'idols must die, so that symbols may live'.

(VI) Jurgen Habermas (B. 1929)

He was German Philosopher who believes that there is a drive in man to dominate nature and human beings. He distinguished 'life world' and systems. 'Life world' is understood as the locus of moral—practical knowledge or relations of meaning shared in families and work place (private) and in political actions and opinions (public). For Habermas, mutual understanding is the telos of human speech—a rational society is committed to achieve this end. He speaks of linguistic competence—mastery of language. Ideal speech, for him, is understood as symmetrical inter subjectivity or is the idea of equivalence between individual. Language, in his view, has the ability to bring mutual understanding—language structure and communication are important (The Cambridge companion to Habermas, edited Stephen K. White, Cambridge: Cambridge University Press, 1995).

He is an influential theorist of socio-critical hermeneutics. According to Anthony Thieselton, Habermas distinguishes between three fundamental cognitive interests: the technical, practical and emancipatory. For Habermas, the approach of the empirical-analytic sciences incorporates a technical cognitive interest; that of the historical hermeneutical sciences incorporates a practical one; the approach of critically-oriented sciences incorporates the emancipatory cognitive interests (*op cit*; p. 382). Habermas finds relationship between hermeneutical understanding and life. He affirms the role of hermeneutics for interpretative or inter-subjective interests, and the goal is interpersonal understanding and social co-operations. For Habermas, the life world should not be reduced to system (scientific aspect) and system should not be reduced to life world. He looks for genuine participation in the life-world.

Habermas is interested in communication. It aims at the formation of a rational consensus among participants as it has to satisfy a number of validity claims—truth, intelligibility and correctness (Josef Bleicher, *The hermeneutic imagination* London: Routledge & Kegan Paul, 1982. p. 33). For Habermas, facts are not entities 'out there', but exists only as correlates of propositions on the level of argumentative reasoning. Their meaning cannot be ascertained outside the process of theoretical discourse. Along with Gadamer, he also states that we can never move outside of the sphere of language (*Ibid.*, p. 34).

(VII) Husserl and Phenomenology

Edmund Husserl is known as Czecho-Austro-German mathematician turned philosopher. Moravia was formerly part of Habsburg or Austro-Hungarian empire and is now Prostejov in the Czech Republic. Edmund Husserl (1859-1938) is the founder of phenomenology. He was born in Moravia, educated in Vienna and Berlin. Phenomenon is appearing of things without a mediation of consciousness. Husserl was not sure of the existence of God or world.

When it is sensed by senses, it is inferred that the world exists. Phenomenology is based on the fundamental distinction between what something is in for itself to us (noumenon) and the manner in which it presents itself (phenomenon). Noumenon is both different and identical with phenomenon.

Husserl was dissatisfied with mathematics as he found that theoretical foundations of modern science is disintegrating. The reason for this disintegration was the existence of an excessively narrow view of empiricism prejudiced in favour of a particular data. So he was for a new empiricism-phenomenlogy. It is the art of disclosing and describing reality as it exists. His main work was 'Logical investigation'. Husserl's phenomenology is the science of the essence of consciousness. It is the medium of existence (David Wodruff Smith, *Husserl*, London: Routledge; 2007. p. 56). Consciousness consists in own experience of seeing, thinking and imagining (*Ibid.*, p. 56). Language, for him, expresses sense as meaning states Smith (*Ibid.*, p. 56).

According to David Wordruff Smith, Husserl's philosophy considers the following things:

(1) Our own conscious experience, especially its intentionality or the way our experiences represent things is the world around us.
(2) The categories of things in the world in general, including individuals, their properties and relations.
(3) Language, as a tool to express our thoughts about the world.

(4) Culture, including social or inter-subjective practices (*Ibid.*, p. 42).

The phenomenologcal knowledge, for him, is related to consciousness and intentionality. His theory of intentionality means meanings are contents of conscious experience, and his theory of knowledge means propositions are contents of judgement (*Ibid.*, p. 72). Kant understands phenomenon as things that appears in our experience. Husserl was exploring the sense or meaning things have in an experience. He also formed a transcendental phenomenology which explores the space of meaning in our lived experience (*Ibid.*, p. 79). For him, it is to interpret and understand the intentionality or sense of meaning of things which we see around us.

(D) Current Perspectives in Hermeneutics

(i) The Reader-Response in Interpretation

The recent hermeneutics shifted its attention from the author to the text (semiotic theory) and also to the reader as the locus of meaning.

G.R. Osborne observes the following things. The reader-response critics posit the union of text and reader at the moment of response. The "author" of a text is a creation of the reader rather than inherent in the text. The text itself exists only in the readers mind, in the sense that the text only takes on life as formal literary entity when the printed page and the reader converge. The moderate position of W. Iser states that the text play a mediating role in guiding as well as correcting the interpreter's understanding. Radical view of S. Fish states that reading community dominates the text, which does not truly exist apart from the reader. For Iser, the reader completes the text's meaning; for Fish the reader creates its meaning. ("Hermeneutics/Interpreting Paul" *Dictionary of Paul and his letters*, p. 389).

According to McKnight, Reader-Response criticism views literature in terms of readers and their values, attitudes and responses. The nature and role of the reader varies in the different forms of reader-response criticism, but in all forms there is a movement away from the view of interpretation as the determination by an autonomous reader of the meaning of an autonomous text. Reader-Response criticism is an attempt to situate a literary work within the cultural context of its production and then explore the shifting relations between the context and the changing contexts of historical readers ("Literary criticism" *Dictionary of Jesus and the Gospels*, p. 476).

(ii) Sociological Reading

The texts are today socio-politically read. This is very much found in the context of liberation hermeneutics. Norman Gottwald in 'The Tribes of Yahweh' made a thorough sociological approach in his study of the people of Israel. It is observed that sociological reading is important because scientific study of Bible requires the knowledge of the social conditions in which traditions are recorded in the Bible (*The Interpretation of the Bible in the Church*, Bangalore: NBCLC, 1994. p. 57). The social sciences and their tools are being used in hermeneutical attempts today. It is recognized that Biblical traditions bore the mark of socio-cultural milieu which transmitted them, so the sociological approach to the Biblical texts has become an integral part of exegesis (*Ibid.*, p. 58). It deals with the various forms of social and religious organization of Israel, the tribal league, the monarchy, the economic and military structure.

In the exegesis of the NT, the questions are related to the life adopted by Jesus and his disciples before Easter, their life style as the members of Jesus movement, the social condition of Pauline communities and social conditions of early Christian communities (*Ibid.*, pp. 58-59). It is also observed that the knowledge of sociological data which helps us to understand the economic, culture and religious functioning of the Biblical world and they are indispensable for historical criticism (*Ibid.*, p. 59).

The Latin America Liberation theologians used the social analytical tools (e.g. marxian analysis) in their approach. The sociological reading is very much found in the hermeneutics of Black theology, dalit theology and other subaltern/contextual theologies.

(iii) Socio-Historical Approach

The socio-historical approach considers the social and historical setting of an event or text. It considers the dynamics of culture, socio-economic and political factors. The dynamic of religion is also an important factor. This study is socio-scientific and also evolutionary. The social science are playing an important role in this approach. It is analytical and reflective. Hegelian and Marxian dialectics (historical dialectics of Hegel and material dialectics of Karl Marx) deal with the struggle in history by the opposite groups. For Karl Marx, history is a history of class struggle. In social historical method, the study of history of the social life of different groups and their kind of relationship is crucial.

This socio-historical approach is related to conflict theory of Karl Marx and it is a sociological and anthropological study. The dynamics and undercurrents are considered. The whole life-setting is even studied from the 'underside' of history. It is a highly critical approach questions the systemic violence, domination, the inequalities and the discriminations. Some of the concepts and practices are prejudiced (e.g. caste system, patriarchy), but this is to re-interpreted as they manifest the selfish motives of the powerful groups to dehumanize others.

The socio-historical study of text or event will help to understand the site of the event, practice or the text which enables us to understand the reality. The text (Biblical text, other scriptures, or any other text) has its own context which is reflecting the socio-historical reality, which has to be critically explored and examined in the hermeneutical process.(Refer Joseph Bleicher, *The Hermeneutic Imagination*).

(iv) Socio-Rhetorical Approach

Vernon K. Robbins is the proponent of socio-Rhetorical interpretation. "Socio-Rhetorical criticism" according to Robbins is an approach to literature that focuses on values, convictions and beliefs both in the texts are read and in the world in which live (Vernon K. Robbins, *Exploring the Texture of Texts*, Pennsylvania: Trinity Press' International, 1996. p. 1) 'Socio' refers to the resources of modern anthropology and sociology that socio-rhetorical criticism brings to the interpretation of the text, states Robbins (*Ibid.*, p. 1). Socio-Rhetorical approach makes use of the elements of the socio-scientific approach which studies the social class, social systems, personal and community status, people on the margins and people in positions of power (*Ibid.*, p. 1). These insights are used in this approach as the exegesis of the text is done.

'Rhetorical' refers to the way language in a text is a means of communication among people. Rhetorical analysis and interpretation give special attention to the subjects and topics a text uses to present thought, stories and arguments. Socio-Rhetorical criticism integrates states Robbins the way people use language with the ways they live in the world (*Ibid.*, p. 1). Socio-Rhetorical criticism brings together literary criticism, rhetorical criticism, post-modern criticism and theological criticism into an integrated approach (*Ibid.*, pp. 1-2).

According to Robbins, interpretation is guided by the insight that language is a means of negotiating meanings in and among the worlds in which people live. He continues to say that this means interpreters are also asked to become aware of their own social location and personal interests the text embodies (*Ibid.*, p. 2). Robbins opines that socio-rhetorical criticism approaches the text as though it were a thickly textured tapestry. As it is found in intricately woven tapestry, a text contains complex patterns and images. This method enables the interpreter to bring multiple textures of the text into view. He exhibits five angles to explore multiple textures within the text: (a) inner texture, (b) Inter-texture, (c) social and cultural texture, (d) ideological texture and, (e) sacred texture (*Ibid.*, pp. 2-3).

Inner Texture is concerned of features like the repetition of particular words, the creation of beginnings and endings, alternation of speech and story telling, particular ways in which the words present arguments, and the particular "feel" or aesthetic of the text. Socio-rhetorical criticism brings together the literary and rhetorical techniques to analyse aspects of words and meaning in the text, states Robbins (*Ibid.*, p. 3). There are six kinds of inner texture in text. They are repetitive, progressive, opening-middle-closing, narrational, argumentative and sensory-aesthetic textures (*Ibid.*, p. 7). According to Robbins, "Repetitive texture resides in the occurrence of words and phrases more than once in a unit. When the same word occurs at least twice in a text, the result is repetition. Multiple occurrences of many different kinds of grammatical, syntactical, verbal or topical phenomena may produce repetitive texture" (*Ibid.*, p. 8). It can be repetition of words like king, resurrection, suffering, or pronouns like 'I', 'you', 'we'. The interpreter closely examines these words and concepts. The progressive texture resides in sequences or progressions of words or phrases throughout the unit (*Ibid.*, p. 10). It discloses the way in which particular idea or concepts are developed in a text. The narrational texture resides in voices through which the words in texts speak. The narrator may introduce people who act and the people who speak. It reveals some kind of pattern that move the discourse programmatically foreword (*Ibid.*, p. 15). In Robbins view, "opening-middle-closing texture resides in the nature of the beginning, body and conclusion of a section of discourse" (*Ibid.*, p. 19). This will help to find out the unit of text. Argumentative texture explores the multiple kinds of inner reasoning in the discourse. The discourse presents assertions and supports them with reasons, clarifies them through opposites and contraries, and possibly presents short or elaborate counter-arguments (*Ibid.*, p. 21). According to Robbins, "The sensory-aesthetic texture of a text resides prominently in the range of senses the text evokes or embodies (thought, emotion, sight, sound, touch, smell) and the manner in which the text evokes or embodies them (reason, intuition, imagination, humour, etc)" (*Ibid.*, pp. 29-30). It provides tone and colour to the discourse.

The *Intertexture* concerns, states Robbins, a text's configuration of phenomena that lie outside the text. Oral-scribal intertexture is concerned of the specific use of language in other texts and people's use of language in daily speech. Social intertexture deals the phenomena like the clothes people wear, the structure of families and households, political arguments, military activities, and distribution of food, money, and services. Cultural intertexture concerns the modes of understanding and belief, like the ideas people have about their importance, their opportunities and their responsibilities in the word. Historical intertexture is concerned of events that occur outside of texts and become historical accounts by means of narrative discourse. Interpreter looks at phenomena outside and inside the text to be interpreted (*Ibid.*, p. 3).

Social and cultural texture should not be confused with social and cultural intertexture. It concerns the potentiality of the text to support social reform, withdrawal, or opposition and to evoke cultural perception of dominance, subordinance, difference, or exclusion. It provides resources for changing people and social practices, for destroying and recreating social order. Cultural categories in the text exhibit the range and values and the priority certain people give to right, lawful or to holy. It produces a particular social and cultural locations to them. The result of the locations is the establishment of dominant, subordinate and marginal cultures within any locale or region. Analysis and interpretation of the social and cultural texture, in Robbins view, explores the range of social orientation and locations in the discourse and the manner in which it relates these orientations and locations of one another (*Ibid.*, pp. 3-4).

Ideological texture is concerned of particular alliances and conflicts the language in a text and the language in an interpretation evoke and nurture. It is also concerned of the way the text itself and interpreters of the text position themselves in relation to other individuals and groups. The issue is the nature of the "particular view itself", states Robbins, that the language evokes and nurtures. Different ideological ranges of texture exist in anthropological, feminist, theological and historical modes of discourse. According to Robbins, "Interpretative discourse itself then takes an interpreter into ideological issues concerning the nature of text itself, the manner in which a text may evoke different points of view, the nature of interpretation, and the nature of the relation of any one interpreter to other interpreters" (*Ibid.*, p. 4).

Sacred texture in texts address the relation of the humans to the divine. Biblical texts contain the sacred texture. Other scriptures also possess sacred texture. According to Robbins, "sacred texture exists in communication about gods, holy persons, spirit beings, divine history, human redemption, human commitment, religious community, and ethics. Analysis of sacred texture is a way systematically probing dynamics across a spectrum of relationships between the human and the divine" (*Ibid.*, p. 4).

The socio-rhetorical criticism challenges the interpreters to explore a text in a systematic, plentiful environment of interpretation and dialogue. "It also presupposes meaning themselves have their meanings by their relation to other meanings", states Robbins. It also provides a wider space and possibilities to investigate and interpret the text (*Ibid.*, p. 4). It helps to analyse and understand the text from different angles.

(v) Literary Approach

Erich Auerbach (1892-1957) was a pioneer of modern literary criticism. His classic work was 'Mimesis' (1947) which holds that gospels stand out as a literature because of the depth of their realism. Hans Wilhelm Frei (1929-89) in his work 'the eclipse of Biblical narrative' (1974) made a significant contribution to literary study of the Bible. His argument is that Bible is 'realistic' in its portrayal of events, even when the events are not 'historical' by modern criteria. According to him, the scholars have ignored the realism as a literary device and missed the message by mistaking it for history. Literary 'realism' does justice to the narrative quality of the text.(Gerald Bray, *Biblical Interpretation: past and present*, Illinois: Intervarsity Press, 1996. pp. 467-468).

The new literary criticism understands the scripture as a literature. It was a reaction against traditional historical critical method. It asserted the autonomy of the text. The text is, for them, independent of the original context so the author's intention is not important. The narrative criticism is very related to literary criticism. It is concerned of the implied author and implied reader. The literary critical implication are taken into account in literary interpretation. The Rhetorical interpretation is also related to the literary interpretation.

According to Gerald Bray, the new literary criticism was developed in 1920's by I. A Richards and T.S. Elliot in the field of literature. They abandoned the history as a model and insisted that work of art must be judged primarily on aesthetic grounds. It examines the intention of the author in writing (author-centred criticism). It is also exploring the inner composition of the text (Text-centred criticism). New literary criticism concentrates also on reader-centred criticism which emphasizes the reader and his or her perception of text (*Ibid.*, pp. 483-484).

The literary criticism, according to Bray, has relative indifference to historical questions. It gives only little value to source, form and redaction criticism. Literary critics are concerned of the final state of the text and its literary effect on readers (*Ibid.*, p. 484).

According to Jones Muthunayagom, the historical critical methods seek the meaning of the text in socio-historical context. In his words, "They try to find out whether the event reported in the Bible actually happened or was it the outcome of the imagination of the author" ("Contemporary approaches to old Testament interpretation" *Interweaving methodology and praxis exploring disciplinary options in today's world* edited by Indukuri John Mohan Razu, Bangalore. SATHRI/BTESSC, 2007. p. 184). B.S. Childs and James Muilenberg raise questions about the traditional historical critical method, so they opt for new literary criticism. The new approach argues that text has a life of its own, independent of its original socio-historical setting (*Ibid.*, p. 184). In the words of Jones Muthunayagom, "Accordingly, the text is autonomous, it has its own meaning, and it must be interpreted exclusively in its own terms. Hence, the original intention of the author for the new criticism is unimportant" (*Ibid.*, p. 185). This approach is very closer to post-modern hermeneutical perspective. The new literary criticism has the elements of post structuralism.

According to Jones Muthunayagom, the new literary critics believe that the Bible is to be understood by the same methods which are used for other literature. They are concerned of identifying the genre, stories, myths and legends. It also analyses the style and literary forms within the text-sentence, structure and metaphor. They are also very much concerned of the intrinsic aspects of the text such as language, words, phrases, syntax, grammar, literary style and plot development (*Ibid.*, p. 185).

(vi) Post-Modern Hermeneutics

Modernism gave importance to reason which was the watch word of enlightenment. Modernity emphasized the humanism, the rationality and knowledge. According to Brian D. Ingraffia, "Whereas modernism tried to elevate man into God's place, post-modern theory seeks to destroy or deconstruct the very place and attributes of God" *(Post-Modern Theory and Biblical Theology; Vanquishing God's shadow*, Cambridge; Cambridge University Press, 1995. p. 1).

Ihab Hassan understands 'immanence' and 'indeterminacy' as characterizing post-modern age. Immanence is the capacity of mind to generalize itself in the world, to act upon both self and world and to its own environment. Indeterminacy relates to heterodoxy, pluralism, eclecticism, randomness, revolt, deformation (Craig Bertholomew, "post/Late? Modernity as the context for Christian Scholarship today" Themelios Vol. 22:2 (January. 1997), p. 26). According to Jean-Francois Lyotard, the post-modern condition is characterized by incredulity toward metanarratives. Metanarratives are those large narratives that undergirded and legitimated the knowledge enterprises in modernity (*Ibid.*, p. 28). The grand narratives are not given validity by post-modernism. The proponent of deconstruction, Jacques Derrida, became an important name in post-Modernism. He promoted, states Craig Betholomew, the idea that language is the bottom-line of reality, textual instability and the inability of language to represent reality accurately. Derrida understands language as 'writing' is the bottom-line of reality and criticized Saussure's privileging of spoken over written language (*Ibid.*, p. 29).

Fragmentation, transience and pluralism are understood as the features of post-modernism. Craig Bertholomew observes that post-modernity has raised all sorts of questions about our capacity to know and how we know and whether we can accurately represent reality (*Ibid.*, p. 31). In post-modernism, according to David Harvey tradition is challenged and looked for change.

It is noted that one of Lyotard's terms 'anagogy' is important for the readers of the Bible. It is described as a interpretation of a word, passage, of text (as of scripture or poetry) that finds beyond the literal, allegorical, and moral sense and a fourth and ultimate spiritual or mystical sense. Anagogy designates a global meaning, not quite reducible to this or that particular part or "Kernel" of truth, not something that can stand in place of something else, but a whole way of looking at phenomena, a "take" on experience charged with its "aura", its power in which the subjects of experience are not so much in possession of their experience, as they are swept up in our experience or understanding that stakes a powerful claim upon them (*The post-modern Bible Reader* edited by David Jobling, Tina Pippin, Ronald Schleifer, Oxford; Blackwell Publishers, 2001. pp. 2-3).

Lyotard argues for delegitimation of the grand narratives of culture, accounts of phenomena that aims at 'totalization' (*Ibid.*, p. 8). Michel Foucault describes the different modes of controlling, selecting, organizing and redistributing discourse. These modes takes three forms such as exterior control, internal control and the social appropriation of discourse. He talks about three kinds of external control. The first one is discursive taboos, the second one is exclusion rather than prohibition, the non-sensical are excluded. The third one is the opposition between true and false. The interior controls also have three dimensions in Foucault's approach. Commentary, which creates a division between primary and secondary texts and aims at the recovery of (authoritative) meaning. The "author-function" or "author position" which imposes identity upon "disturbing language" by identifying its unit, coherence and the manner of its "insertion in the real" and disciplines, which control the production of statements by defining the objects, methods, and propositions of particular disciplinary discourses such as biology, history, philosophy or the "theoretical horizon" of knowledge (*Ibid.*, p. 10).

Walter Benjamin talks about translation in an intertextual way, as one text illuminates another text. For him translation should be literal and not as something that resembles the meaning of the original. Translation must, in his words, incorporate the original's mode of signification. For Benjamin, the value of the text in translation lies in its confrontation with the original text, not in its infallible transmission of meaning. In translation, the original is brought to life and the "pure language" imprisoned within the original text is "liberated". In his words, the literal translation harmoniously supplements and complements the original text. Literalness and freedom are united in Benjamin's understanding. In his view on translation, it is said, the text is perpetually incomplete, never entirely possessed or possessable (*Ibid.*, p. 14). Literal translation does not guarantee an accurate meaning of the text, but Benjamin hopes that it will inspire the reader back to the original text. (*Ibid.*, p. 14).

Frederic Jameson, the American Marxist critic talks about three stages or horizons. The first one is the individual text within its specific political context. It is related to deconstruction. The interpreter identifies the text's basic "contradiction", the point where its attempt to create a coherent world of meaning most conspicuously fails, and then attempts to correlate this contradiction with some contradictory feature of the society. The second horizon, that of "class struggle" moves beyond the individual text to a reading of as many texts as possible that are contemporaneous with it to know how the different choices are available are related to class division in the society. The third horizon is based on the perspective that the context for the individual text is nothing else than the whole of world history as understood in Marxist theory, which creates the possibility of "anagogic" understanding. The mode of production (e.g. Feudal, capitalist and communist) are important here. Texts, for him, represents "fields of force" within these conflicts between modes of production (*Ibid.*, p. 20).

The different political consciousness are found in the Bible also as we see the dominant modes of production (Egypt, Greek, Rome, Mesapotamia etc.), at the same time Prophets task for egalitarianism and the early church's sharing. The slave-master differences in Rome and Greece are also to be noted. It is said that these create rich potential for the reading of the Biblical texts as site of conflict between different "political consciousness" (*Ibid.*, p. 21) Jameson as a Marxist is affirming the hermeneutical privilege of the working class from the framework of class struggle. For Jameson, Marxism contains always the post-modern elements (*Ibid.*, p. 21).

There can be some specific hermeneutical principles one can draw from the post-modern thinking.

(1) Deconstruction is one of the important aspect in Derrida. It can be also called de-legitimation or iconoclasm. It goes beyond the existing understanding, perspectives and notions. It is post-structural in nature. It challenges grand or metanarratives. It is a perspective of differance. There is de-legitimation of dominant structure and their values.

(2) Reader-Response is another significant aspect in post-modern hermeneutics. The author and context are not important. It affirms the death of the author. The meaning of the text is solely based on the readers and their responses. In a sense, people in the context and their understanding about the text is important than the intended meaning of the author. This idea one may find in Jacques Derrida.

(3) It is based on the de-centering principles, as it is non-hierarchical and non-authoritarian in nature. The post-modern hermeneutics does not approve the voices of the traditional structures of hierarchy or authority. It does not affirm any centre. The meaning of the text cannot be dictated by any hegemonic powers. The centres of authority is in question, so also their interpretations and understanding of reality.

(4) Concern for the marginated or subalterns is another principle. Foucault challenges the hegemonic power. He also gives importance to the 'other' or the marginalized. He was very conscious how the mainstream society alienate the sick, disabled and powerless. He gave the example of how lepers are treated by the structures of hierarchy and authority. They are dispossessed and chased out by family, the ruling authority and whole society. Post-modernism goes against victimization. It is liberative in nature. It questions structures such as patriarchy and capitalism. It empowers the disempowered.

(5) Post-modern hermeneutics affirms pluralism. It goes against monolithic structures and homogeneity and it affirms heterogeneity. It affirms it based on fragmentation, relativity and rapidity. The particularities are important for post-modernism than what is universalized and generalized.

(6) Re-imagining/Re-imaging is another principle. Radical re-thinking or perspectival change is found in post-modern thought. It is anti-foundational,

anti-totalizing anti-pyramidical and anti-structural. Text may find meaning only in a posterior sense. No prior determination or fixation of meaning is possible. There is an epistemic shift taking place as against the existing traditional interpretative methods. New awareness about reality lead to new meaning of the text. There is re-imagining of existing philosophies, theologies, ideologies, values and structures

(viii) Post-Colonial Hermeneutics

Post-colonialism deals with the orient and it challenges the colonial notions and perspectives. In colonialism, the 'other' is not important, but in post-modernism and postcolonalism there is re-imagining or reviewing of the perspective on the other. The other is the marginated ones who play significant roles in history. The poststructural/ post-modern elements like deconstruction or delegitmation is found in post-colonial interpretation. The aspects like orientalism, contrapuntal, hybridity are very much stressed by certain post-colonial thinkers in their interpretation. The post-colonial hermeneutics has to identify the oppressive and dehumanizing elements and resist and re-interpret them, as it finds them in the dominant, elitistic, western and colonial interpretations. The post-colonial hermeneutics should have the following characteristics.

(1) It is post-structural. Post-colonial reading is post-structural in character. The texts can have 'meaning'

beyond the meaning. Here the post-modernism also play an important role, as the text is to be re-structured or deconstructed. The colonial reading which is distorted and oppressive has to be deconstructed. Here the reader play a vital role in the re-reading. Post-colonial reading is a challenge to the structures of domination. Post-colonial hermeneutics focusses on identifying the structures which projects and supports the imperial, dominant or oppressive spirit and to resist and de-legitimize them. The counter elements or what is contrapuntal or resisting the colonial spirit is also very crucial here.

(2) It is contextual or indigenous in character. The principle of contextuality plays a significant role in post-colonial hermeneutics. Post-colonialism is a resistance to colonialism and its thinking. The decolonizing process is coming back to the roots. It affirms the nativity or indigeneity. The spirit of indigeneity or contextuality is found in third world hermeneutics and theology. Asian/Indian and Latin American theologies and hermeneutics consider the contextuality very seriously. It recognizes the experiences, values, historical struggles of the oppressed and colonized humanity. Biblical text has to be interpreted not on the basis of imported or western ideology and theology, but on the basis of the contextual experiences of the people. It has to consider the socio-economic and political reality of the oppressed or colonized people.

(3) There is liberative character is post-colonial hermeneutics. It challenges or critically looks at the colonial and oppressive structures. It goes against the tides. It challenges the legitimization of the oppression and domination. It is conflictual in nature. It has dissenting voice against injustice and exploitation. It sides the marginelized like poor, dalits, tribals, blacks victimized, women and other oppressed or subaltern groups. It is a dynamic process in the interpretation of the scripture. Scripture is interpreted with a liberative motif, as it recongnizes the struggle of the oppressed. It also considers the historical and sociological realities. The aspect of liberation is found in the third world reading of the text. Feminist, dalit, tribal and black and other liberative hermeneutics considers the importance of radical restructuring in the concepts, structures value system and perspectives. It aims at the liberation.

According to C.I. David Joy the post-colonial analysis of the text I reading will expose the following:

(1) The colonial motifs hidden in text.
(2) The colonial intentions of the interpreters of the text.
(3) An alternative way for monologic reading.
(4) Native cultures as they are taken into account.
(5) Reading as it becomes a gesture of resistance ('Historical Jesus Research: A Post-colonial Cultural Reconstruction' *Bangalore Theological Form*, vol.

XLl, No. 2, (December 2009), p. 88). David Joy also quotes from the article "Biblical criticism and post-colonial studies" by Fernando Segovia, who talks about three foci which are to be noted in the process of post-colonial reading. They are as follows:

(1) Analysing the texts that emerged in the imperial contexts.

(2) Analysing the readings and interpretations of the texts during the colonial period.

(3) Understanding of the Socio-Political milieu of the readers of the texts who lived in the reality of empire, imperialism and colonialism (*Ibid.*, p. 89).

According to Sugirtharajah, "colonial reading can be summed up as informed by theories concerning the innate superiority of western culture, the western male as subject and the natives, heathens, women, blacks, indigenous people, as the other, needing to be controlled and subjugated" (R.S. Sugirtharaja "Biblical studies after the empire: From a colonial to a post-colonial mode of interpretation" *The Bible and post-colonialism*, I edited by R.S. Sugirtharajah, Sheffield: Sheffield Academic Press, 1998. p. 16). He continues to state that this domineering spirit in reading practice has to be challenged. In his view what post-colonialism does is to enable us to question the totalizing tendencies of European reading practices and interpret the texts on our own terms and read them from our specific locations" (*Ibid.*, p. 16). The contextual, post-structuralist and liberative aspect of post-colonial hermeneutics is affirmed by Sugirtharajah.

V

Post-Modern and Post-Colonial Theology

1. Post-Modern Theology

Nietzsche's philosophical ideas have influenced the secular or radical and even the post-modern theologies. One can find traces of post-modernity in death of God theology and process theology. Certain post-modern trends are found in theologies of the marginated like the liberation theology, dalit theology, black theology and feminist theology.

Post-modernism affirms the nihilism (Nietszche), chaos, uncertainty, absolute relativism, rapidity, localism and pluralism. It rejects any centre and also the fixity. Traditional understanding of structure and form (e.g. arts, architecture and literature) are questioned and deconstructed (Jacques Derrida's deconstruction) The concepts such as God and faith are radically deconstructed in process thought and also in death of God theology. This post-modern trend is also found in the Biblical hermeneutics. It affirms the 'death of the author' as what is meant by the author is not important, but the way in which the reader understands is important.

God is no more at the centre, as He is absent or eclipsed and faith and religion are not necessary for the present world. So the absolute relativistic understanding is found in secular theology like death of God and also in post-modern thought. The humanism is also challenged (man is no more at the centre) by post-modernism. The counter-culture (Sebastian Kappen) and non-legitimation (dalit theology—A.P. Nirmal) are closely related to post-modern thinking. The openness towards liberation, people (people-oriented), pluralism and localism in theology are also having post-modern spirit. The critical and creative or positive use of post-modern elements in theologizing can be affirmed, and the extreme and negative aspects should be rejected.

A radical deconstruction is in process in theology. There is a movement from modern to post-modern in all aspects of life including philosophy, theology and culture. No theology can be, however, formulated by rejecting God, faith and the values, but the task can be a re-conceiving to have the essence or original understanding.

According to Clayton Crockett, in the 1980's, an initial post-modern theology developed around the work of Mark C. Taylor, Charles E. Winquist, Carl A. Raschke and other, which combined insights into the situation of the death of God with contemporary continental philosophy. An important collection appeared in 1982, called *Deconstruction and Theology*, which included essays by Altizer, Taylor, Winquist, Raschke and Robert p. Scharlemann. In his influential book (1984) titled 'Erring', Taylor set forth four themes of post-modern a theological thinking, including the death of God, the disappearance of the self, the end of history and the closure of the book. Such works set an agendas for the radical theological inquiry ("Introduction" *Secular Theology. American radical theological thought,* edited by Clayton Crockett, London: Routledge, 2001. p. 5).

Charles E. Winquist explains the notion of post-modern theology as follows; "The notion of post-modern theology does not entail a specific agenda but is more importantly a thinking theologically that accounts for the conditions under which we think that are themselves indexical marks of the post-modern condition. Post-modernity cannot be simply dated and the post-modern is not synonymous with the contemporary. There are instead distinctive traits of a post-modern sensibility that call for theological understanding and thereby characterize the meaning and possibilities for post-modern theological thinking" ("Post-modern Secular Theology" *secular theology*. p. 26).

Winquist states again that, "the publication of *The Alchemy of the word* (Raschke. 1979), *Deconstruction and Theology* (Altizer *et al.* 1982 (and especially *Erring: A post-modern A theology* (Taylor 1984) brought the deconstructive philosophy of Jacques Derrida into the arena of theological discourse" *(Ibid.*, p. 26). Nietzsche, Marx and Freud did contribute to the post-modern environment. Marx, according to Winquist, emphasized the materiality of history; Freud, the materiality of the body; and Nietzsche, the materiality of language (*Ibid.*, p. 26-27). The influences of Jacques Lucan, Jean Francios Lyotard, Julia Kristeva, Giles Deleuze, Michel Foucault and Paul

Ricoeur in post-modern thinking, hermeneutics, ethics and theology are to be recognized (*Ibid.*, p. 26).

In the early post-modern theology, 'Deconstruction' and 'Death of God' are celebrated as an influence for new thinking. Winquist observes that Taylor's publication of 'Erring' was a manifesto for a deconstructionist post-modern theology deeply influenced by radical theology and Derrida. Taylor claims that deconstruction is the 'hermeneutic' of the death of God. Raschke claims that deconstruction is in the final analysis, the death of God put into writing (*Ibid.*, p. 27). Post-modern theology moves against the totalization of thinking and it is commitment to an extraordinary discourse states Winquist. He points out that "A recent theme in post-modern philosophical and theological thinking has been the return of religion, but it is a religion without religion" (*Ibid.*, p. 30). Derridas' view of religion without religion can lead to a theology without religion, states Winquist.

The process thought argues that everything is subject to change and is relative so reality is a process. The concept of the absolute and immutable are not recongnized by process thought. It stands for changeability and contingency. The evolutionary hypothesis is also found in process thought. These elements are found in post-modern theology also.

The Post-modern theology is the offshoot of a radical theology and its shape and nature are beyond any imagination. According to Victor E. Taylor, post-modern theology transforms shape into shapelessness, with shape refigured as "disbecoming" ("Theography: signs of God in a post-modern age", *Secular Theology*, p. 193). Post-modern theologians Raschke and Mark C. Taylor argue for a theology that is emancipated from the metaphysical discourse *(Ibid.*, p. 193). Post-modern theologians like Crockett understands God as a sign among other signs (*Ibid.*, p. 206). God is represented as power without (total) knowledge, as power is decentralized and "deconstructed", States Peter Canning ("God is of possibility" *Secular Theology*, p. 236).

The meta or grand narratives are challenged by Lyotard and post-structuralism and so also post-modernism. The totalizing is rejected, so also foundationalism. There is also de-legitimation and decentering of power and knowledge. The heterogeneous aspects, pluralism and contextuality or localism are emphasized by post-modernism. It also stressed the particulars rather than the generalized and universal 'facts'. The hegemonic forces are also challenged.

So in post-modern theology there is room to do theology from the perspective of dalits, the tribals, blacks, women and other subaltern/marginalized people. Post-modernism has radically challenged the grand narratives found in the form of patriarchy, caste hierarchy, capitalism, western theology and Marxism. There is space for empowerment for the disempowered, and to deconstruct and de-legitimize the discriminatory and enslaving systems and structures. There is possibility for a different and particular theology in post-modernism. It empowers and liberates the people of the margins. Hegemony like the Brahminic dominance, male-domiance or the dominance of the whites or west are not accepted by post-modernism, which is also providing a room for making a theology from the oppressive situation for the victimized people.

Post-modernism provides complete possibility to revise and deconstruct what is dehumanizing and oppressive. The formalistic and structuralist view of the divine power, knowledge, authority, narrations and frameworks are to be challenged in order to formulate a post-modern perspective of theology. The hierarchical and hegemonic understanding of power is also not emancipatory. But the elements such as disorder or chaos, nihilism and anarchy cannot be given importance as we critically use post-modern tools.

2. Post-Colonial Theology

Homi K. Bhabha refers to post-colonial as the form of social criticism that bears witness to the unequal and uneven process of representation by which the historical experience of the once colonized third World came to be framed in the west, states Padmini Mongia (*Contemporary post-colonial Theory A: Reader* edited by Padmini Mongia, London: Arnold, 1997. p. 1).

Post-colonialism points the effects of colonialism that impacted the structures and thought, and it looks foreword the deconstruction in the area of history, art, literature, philosophy and sociology. It challenges the colonial-imperialistic patterns of thought and actions and made a liberative attempt to redeem them from the distorted perspective of the west.

The colonizers (western countries) have been challenged politically, culturally and ideologically by decolonized countries. The western power, knowledge and methodology are questioned by the colonized as they organized themselves to struggle against the dominance of the west. Though it began early, the organized form of post-colonial thought was developed as freedom of power (political independence) and freedom of thought in the19th century. The people movements which are also liberative movements which affirm the dignity, identity and rights are the vehicles of Post-colonial ideology. The liberation theology, women theology, Black theology, dalit theology, tribal theology and minjung theology which are known as subaltern theologies and the effort such as contextualization/inculturation are the influence of the post-Colonial ethos.

Post-colonial theory is emerged out of the new socio-historic pressure as it is found that the new social movements around the issues such as race, gender and ethnicity have revealed the limits of older conceptions about community, individuals and nation (*Ibid.*, p. 5). Pre-colonial is interested in re-writing history in terms of the stages such as pre-colonial, colonial and post-colonial (*Ibid.*, p. 7). Post-colonial thought looks to what is 'native' and also looks forward as it challenges dominant, imperialistic world-view. It is a re-reading or re-interpretation of history, methodology, theology and sources (e.g. scripture). As against the western, colonial, elitistic perspectives, the post-colonial theological and non-theological discourses argue for liberation from Patriarchy, slavery and challenges gender-injustice, human right violations, and different kinds of oppressions. In post-colonial theological discourses, the indigenous or native resources are critically and creatively used as methodology is more experiential, contextual and narrative, and also there is a 'deconstruction' in the whole perspectives. Post-colonialism explores the potentials of the orient. The positive elements in the eastern or third world religions, cultures (in the from of myths, folkores, poetry, songs) and social life (historical consciousness) are explored by post-colonial ideology and theology.

According to Rey Chow, the post-colonialist affirms the resurrection of the native or challenging the dominant discourse by 'resurrecting', the victimized voice ("where have all the Natives Gone?" *Contemporary Post-colonial Theory*: A Reader, edited by Padmini Mongia, p. 129). Nationalism, Sovereignty, Constitutionality, self-reliance, movements towards cultural and religious roots, resistance against gender and racial prejudices and emancipatory thrust are related to post-coloniality. The marginality, third world experience, feminity, Blackness, Asianness and Indianness, native or indigenous expressions in theology are holding the post-colonial character. The theology of the subaltern or the victimized groups are post-colonial in nature as they struggle against the imperial, colonial or oppressive powers.

According to Ruth Frankenberg and Lata Mani, for India post-colonialism means independence from Britain, birth of the nation-state, end of territorial colonialism, economic growth by the growth of indigenous capitalism, non-aligned either the First or second world ("crosscurrents, Crosstalk: Race, 'Post-coloniality' and the politics of Location" *Contemporary post-colonial theory*, p. 347). Post-colonialism means, or Britain the loss of most of their colonies, the appearance on British landscapes of a significant number of people from the former colonies which makes the predominantly white ethnic society into multi-racial society. It also refers to questioning western or white dominance by the movements of resistance and the emergence of struggles for collective determination which is articulated in nationalist terms, states Ruth Frankenberg and Lata Mani (*Ibid.*, p. 348).

According to Musa W. Dube, "Post-colonial theories emanated from the rise of western empires in the eighteenth through the twentieth centuries, their scramble to divide the world among themselves, the strategies of subjugation and resistance engendered by colonialism, and the chain reactions that have been in motion ever since" ("Post-coloniality, Feminist spaces, and Religion" *Post-colonialism, Feminism and Religious Discourses* edited by Laura E. Donaldson & Kwok Puilan, New York: Rutledge, 2002. p. 100).

According to Dube, post-colonial feminisms display a number of reconizable strategies and concerns in their decolonizing and depatriarchalizing practices. She continues to say that post-colonial feminist operates within the past and present international oppression which continues to exert its forms of oppressions in their lives. She also states that they indicate that international opperssion of the former colonies have exerted a greatest influence on colonized women (*Ibid.*, p. 115)

Dube was very conscious of the colonial forces which

subjugated and silenced the women. She argues that the post-colonial feminists in their reading and writing call for the decolonization of inherited colonial educational system, language, literary canons and reading methods. It is also stated that the decolonizing practices of two-thirds world feminists are accompanied by a willingness to embrace and confront indigenous, religious and cultural worldview which include willingness to pronounce legitimate and adequate wherever possible, to interpret them where necessary, and to avoid the colonizing strategy of dismissing as negative all social systems of the colonized (*Ibid.*, pp. 115-116).

Dube asserts that a decolonizing feminist practices also must show how international domination renders women of former colonies politically invisible, economically impoverished, and culturally suppressed while it highlights diverse way of resistance and liberation (*Ibid.*, p. 116). Muse W Dube. insists also that post-colonial feminist strategies must confront oppressive aspects in one's own indigenous systems of gender oppressive practices such as genital mutilation and sati. There are rooms for re-interpreting the old and promoting good as no culture is absolutely negative or wholly pure. In these decolonizing spaces, she states, post-colonial feminist analysis wrestles with the restoration of some aspects of the indigenous cultures and reinterprets others for the empowerment of women and all people (*Ibid.*, p. 116). Post-colonial ideology questions the colonization of women's bodies especially the black, and other marginated women which began in slavery; the brutalizing sexual assault on them is criticized (M. Shawn

Copeland, "Body, representation and Black religious discourse" *Post-colonialism, feminism and Religious Discourse.* p. 182). The discrimination in the name of gender or race is questioned by post-colonialism.

According to R.S. Sugirtharajah, the western modes of scientific thinking whether it is liberal, rational or positivist only can enslave us, so we have to be freed from them. The indigenous or native expressions and thought patterns are to be upheld. (*The Bible and the third world*, Cambridge: Cambridge University Press, 2001, p. 176). The central task of post-colonial biblical interpretation is described as recovery, reoccupation and transcription of one's culture which has been degraded and affected from the colonial narratives and from mainstream Biblical scholarship, states Sugirtharajah (*Ibid.*, p. 177). According to him, "Vernacular hermeneutics tries to erase the painful memory of this degradation and effacement, and to make a fresh start by returning to one's roots. Impelled by a variety of cultural and political forces, it is an attempt to go 'home' It is a call to self-awareness, aimed at creating an awakening among people to their indigenous literary, cultural and religious heritage" (*Ibid.*, p. 177). Vernacular is understood in nativism, cultural nationalism, indigenous, struggle for the historical and political presences of groups suppressed or marginalized by colonization and modernization, an assertion and selfhood and self-respect instead of slavish conformity to received ideas, valuing the indigenous resources and deep distrust of the centralizing tendencies of Euro-American critical theories. (*Ibid.*, p. 177).

The post-colonial intertexual reading is found in the

biblical interpretation. According to Sugirtharajah, the post-colonial interpretation has the vocation to de-ideologizing dominant interpretation and the distrust of the totalizing, tendencies (*Ibid.*, p. 224). Sugitharajah states again, post-colonial theory offers a space for the once colonized. It is an interpretative act of the descendants of those once subjected. In effect, it means a resurrection of the marginal, the indigene and subaltern". (*Ibid.*, p. 250).

The task of the post-colonial criticism, according to Sugirtharajah, is to engage in reconstructive reading of Biblical texts. In his words, 'post-colonial reading will reread Biblical texts from the perspective of post-colonial concerns such as liberation struggles of the past and present; it will be sensitive to subaltern and feminine elements embedded in texts' (*Ibid.*, p. 252).

Post-colonial theology is narrative, liberative, nativistic and people-oriented. It upholds the struggle of the oppressed and goes against the elites or dominant class and the colonizers. There is a re-understanding of theology as post-colonial theology challenges the western thinking and methodology which is more individualistic, capital intensive and imperialistic. Post-colonial theology is concerned of the marginalized or subaltern such as poor, women, blacks, dalits and tribals. It re-reads the scripture in the light of the aspirations of the victimized and also give importance to the indigenous resources. It does value what is native.

The post-colonial theology is also influenced by post-structualism and post-modernism. The aspects such as orientalism, nationalism, indigeneity, and contextuality play vital roles in post-colonial theology. It also deconstructs the traditional, dominant and western forms of ideology and theology. Post-colonial theology challenges the authoritarian structures and it sides the oppressed or marginated. The subaltern experience and their consciousness is also very crucial in post-colonial Theology. Post-colonial theology is also liberative. It challenges patriarchy, caste hierarchy, racial discrimination and hegemony. The empowerment of dalits, tribals, victimized women, blacks and other suffering humanity is an essential concern of post-colonial theology.

VI

Post-Modern and Post-Colonial Ethics

1. Post-Modern Ethics

In ethics and theology changes are taking place because of the changes of the context. There is a movement from colonialism to post-colonialism. The post-colonial situation is now neo-colonial. Now the colonialism is almost come to an end, but we see the fierce emergence of neo-colonialism, which is a new way of exploiting or oppressing the third world by the first world. Now we are also concerned of the movement from modernism to post-modernism. The present era is described as post-modern.

The modernism was a challenge to the traditional ethos. The enlightenment played a crucial role in the emergence of the modern. The importance given to human reason, scientific worldview and the humanism have contributed to modernism. The critical spirit and the freedom of thought and human potentiality are hailed in modernism. The development to science and technology placed man very high. The scientific rationality is developed so the people looked for the autonomy and freedom from religious and social structures. It is critical of what is authoritarian, superstitious and irrational.

The question of 'knowledge' is also very significant in the issue of modernism. 'I believe what can be observed' is positivism, which promotes experimentation in the understanding of knowledge. This view questioned the 'a priori' knowledge and credibility of knowledge furnished by the church, traditional wisdom and dictated morality. The belief, the practices and the understanding of scriptures undergo radical changes. The empirical philosophy was a contribution of David Hume the Scottish Philosopher who holds that knowledge is received through experience (matter of fact experience) rather than religious. It is aposteriori. The speculative medieval theories of knowledge are absurd for Hume and Kant. For Hume knowledge has to be verified by experiment. The intellectual reasoning and the humanism are given at most importance by them which is a significant contribution to modernism.

In post-modernism there is chaos, as there is no authority or norm. The norms and authority are rejected. The word post-modern is first appeared in the 1870s but again it is widely used in the ensuing decades with different shades of meanings. According to Craig Brtholomew, the term Post-modern in 1950s and 60s emerged as a reaction to modernism in the arts. It is later found in the field of literature especially literary criticism. Ihab Hassan proposed the idea of a post-modern literature of silence which is anti-representationalist and anti-modernist in its move towards disorder and attack on form [*Themelios* (January 1975), p. 25]. The indeterminacy (not fixed, vague) also contributed to post-modernity. It is explained that indeterminacy relates to heterodoxy, pluralism eclecticism, randomness revolt and deformation. Immanence and indeterminacy are understood as the heart of post-modern episteme (*Ibid.*, p. 26). The philosophical (ideas) cultural (arts, religion) and social (capitalism, politics, communications) shifts are all ingredients in post-modernism (*Ibid.*, p. 26).

David Lyon sums up the modernity as follows, "modernity is all about the massive changes that took place at many levels from the mid-sixteenth century onwards, changes signalled by the shifts that uprooted agricultural workers and transformed them into mobile industrial urbanites. Modernity questions all conventional ways of doing things substituting authorities of its own, based in science, economic growth democracy or law. And it unsettles the self; if identity is given in traditional society, in modernity it is constructed "(quoted by Craig Bartholomew, *Ibid.*, p. 27). The meaninglessness and aloneness (the society of strangers) and ecological crises becomes the order of the day which contributes to crisis in modernism, and its name is post-modernity. According to Brian D. Ingraffia, "whereas modernism tried to elevate man into God's place, post-modern theory seeks to destroy or deconstruct the very place and attributes of God" *(Post-modern Theory and Biblical Theology: Vanquishing God's Shadow,* p. 1). In post-modernism man is only a tiny being among the realities. Nietschze's transvaluation of values and elimination of God (God is dead) have influenced the post-modernity.

Jurgen Habermas challenged the view that postmodernity is the end of modernity. For him, modernity is an unfinished project. In the view of Jean-Francois Lyotard, post-modern condition is characterized by incredulity (unwilling to believe) towards metanarratives. Metanarratives are those large narratives that undergirded and legitimated the knowledge enterprise in modernity. It is said that legitimation of knowledge always requires some narrative, but, in the post-modern context, such narratives are not credible. The grand narratives have lost its validity. The postmodernity challenged the possibility of the transcendent and the validity of the narratives are made local. There is no consensus, in Lyotard's view on true knowledge [Themelios (January, 1997) p. 28].

Jacques Derrida is famous for his attempts on deconstruction. He tries to dismantle the Judaeo-Christian roots of metaphysics by his deconstruction. In his deconstruction of ontotheology, he considers Christian theology as a prime example of logo centric metaphysics. He also feels that Christian theology is unable to guard against foreign philosophical influences (Brian D. Ingraffia, *Post-modern Theory and Biblical theology*, p. 13).

According to Craig Bartholomew, as Thiselton points out, deconstruction in literary theory is often perceived as the strongest philosophical context of post-modernism and Derrida is one of the exponents (*Ibid.*, p. 29). For Derrida, language is the bottom line of reality and it is unable to represent the reality accurately. In his view, there is also textual instability. For him, writing is prior to speech. Writing is not mere inscription in his view. Writing is related to every system of communication—pictorial, musical and sculptural writing (*Ibid.*, p. 30).

Fragmentation and transience characterize postmodernity accompanied by thorough going pluralism, says Craig Bartholomew (*Ibid.*, p. 30). Derrida does not see any firm grounding of language which is not illusory. In Craig Bartholomew's observation, postmodernity has raised all sorts of questions about our capacity to know and how we know and whether we can accurately represent reality, i.e., about epistemology. The possibility of universal knowledge is considered as impossible and it considers all knowledge to be local, communal and human construct. It also undermined the rationalistic, autonomous view of human which was dominant in modernity. In his view, postmodernity is characterized by pluralism, uncertainty, instability and fragmentation. The old certainties seem to have gone, with no unified vision to replace them (*Ibid.*, p. 32). Postmodernity leads to relativism.

In modernity, the factors like secularization, urbanization and the science and technology have contributed positively and relatively to the society. In the ethical reflection also these factors made greater impact. There was a wise and responsible use of science (knowledge) and also the abuse of science and technology. Man's potentiality and knowledge went even to the extreme to ruthlessly tap the resources and spoil the atmosphere by their industrial enterprise and brought the ecological crises which become a severe threat to survival. At the same time, the irrationality and superstitions were questioned, and humanness was upheld. The traditional value system and religious authority have come under the attack. A new awareness of the reality was emerged which questioned the discrimination and argued for freedom. Modernism was a boon and a bane. If the responsibility is lost, any system or ideology can be a curse. Evaluating the crisis of modernism Dr. K.C. Abraham has said that it is hazardous to life as it is destroying the basic fabric of human relationships.

The neo-colonial forces played a very crucial role to control the economic structure as they appeared in the form of IMF, MNCs and TNCs. It was also a bad effect of modernism. Modernism paved the way for different kinds of developments which were misused by the capitalistic forces. The impact of postmodernity is a very hard issue to discuss with. In globalization, the postmodernity must have an impact. Globalization is a free market consumeristic ideology where the persons are not important, but the products and the money. Man is only a spectator and he is a tiny being among several beings around. The pluralism supports the different experiences and realities and so also the relativism.

The relativism is related to fragmentation and uncertainty which the post-modernism promotes. Homogenization and universalization are being challenged. The ethical norms also undergo radical threat. Ethics will be relativistic or ethics becomes absurd. There is no set standards as everything is uncertain or vague. It nihiliates God so also the ethical norms and value system. There can be misuse of freedom or absolute freedom where nobody is mutually responsible. Post-modernism provides a new culture, a new social structure, a new world-view and a new 'morality' as against the existing and traditional. It is after the new trends in all aspects of life.

Post-modern ethics has the following characteristics:-

(1) The post-modern ethics is people-oriented. It affirms decentralization. It is for openness and decision making is possible as it stands above traditional hierarchy and authority. It regards the 'other' or powerless or the marginated. It challenges the hegemonic forces or structures of domination. It stands for the empowerment of the disempowered. The subaltern groups like poor, dalits, tribals, blacks and victimized women and their emergence is a concern in post-modern ethical perspective.

(2) It is an ethics of deconstruction. Post-modern ethics goes beyond the dominant value and ideological system as it questions the systems and structures that are totalized. The anti-foundational and anti-hierarchical stance of post-modernism challenges the imposed values (e.g.: Marxism, patriarchy, caste system, deontology). It does not approve the superiority claim, dominance or impositions of any value system. It gives freedom to re-imagining as we deconstruct and re-construct the existing values.

(3) Post-modern ethics is contextual. It provides room for people to consider their experiences. Pluralism, contingency, rapidity and fragmentation are recognized by post-modernism. The people and their context play vital roles in post-modernism. The context of the margins or the other (neglected

persons and groups) are given importance by post-modern ethics.

(4) Post-modern ethics is liberative. Post-modern ethics has dealt with people of the margins. It challenges structures of domination or hegemonic forces that oppress them. The power, authority, the 'knowledge' (epistemology) of the dominant and hegemonic imposition of values are questioned by post-modern ethics. It looks for an epistemological shift as it considers the powerless. The liberative spirit is inherent in post-modern ethics. Disregarding the 'other' (marginated) is not approved by post-modern ethics. Post-modern ethics is other-regarding.

2. Post-Colonial Ethics

Post-colonialism challenges the colonialism and it resists the impositions and importation of any value system from the west or from the dominant groups. Neo-colonialism or globalization is the new form of colonization taking place all over the world. The powerless erstwhile colonized countries are badly affected by globalization. Globalization is an imposition of the culture, economic and political policies of the hegemonic forces (Western Countries) over the third world.

Following are the characteristic of post-colonial ethics:

(1) Post-colonial Ethics is Anti-Hegemonic

It is not compromizing with the powerful or the dominant

forces. It is concerned of the issues of the colonized. As we see in post-modernism, it is against the totalizing of the hegemonic forces and their structures. So it is post-structural in nature. The values of the dominant powers and the imposition of their ideologies are rejected by post-colonialism. It questions the oppressive and exploitative elements.

(2) Post-colonial Ethics is Contextual

Post-colonialism affirms the contextuality. The experience of the decolonized or the indigenous people are very significant for post-colonialism. The particular context, the pluralism, the persons and people are considered in contextual ethics. The struggles of the people of the third world and their socio-economic realities and the stark reality of poverty are responded in post-colonial ethics. Post-colonial ethics is praxis-oriented.

(3) Post-colonial Ethics is Liberative

Post-colonial ethics looks for deconstruction as we see in post-modernism. It challenges existing structures of domination (Western or Eastern) and look forward a radical re-restructuring of the society. Spivak was pointing the disregard towards the subaltern. Their identity and crisis are to be taken into account when we deal with post-colonial ethics. The victimized groups need empowerment and liberation. They include dalits, tribals, trans genders, blacks, other indigenous groups and victimized women. Post-colonial ethics is an ethics of the poor, powerless and victimized. It challenges the oppressing and exploitative structures.

The issue of land, nationalism, poverty, women, dalits, tribals, blacks and other marginalized groups and the struggle for equal distribution of resources and empowerment are major concerns in post-colonial theology and ethics. Post-colonial ethics is not rooted in what is classical, western or dominant, but radical as it is indigenous, people-oriented and anti-hegemonic.

Conclusion

Post-modernism and post-colonialism are having their own contexts. Post-modernism is a reaction to modernism and post-colonialism is the situation after colonialism. It is a resistance to colonial spirit. But post-modernism had influenced the post-colonialism. Both are post-structural in character. The elements such as pluralism, localism/contextuality, anti-hegemonical stance, de-centering of power, onsidering the 'other' or marginalized/victimized are the concerns of both post-modernism and post-colonialism. The heterogeneity and indigeneity are also the concerns of both ideologies. Both ideologies are also against grandnarratives and hierarchy. Both are also liberative in nature. The element of deconstruction is also found in post-modernism and post-colonialism.

Post-modernism affirms the nihilism and chaos. It may be also described as chaotic. These elements are not supported by post-colonialism. Both post-modernism and post-colonialism provide ample room for re-thinking and developing a perspective which is empowering the marginated or subaltern as they challenge the structures of domination.

Index